Sentimental Education

Schooling, Popular Culture and the Regulation of Liberty

JAMES DONALD

VERSO

London · New York

First published by Verso 1992
© James Donald 1992
All rights reserved

Verso
UK: 6 Meard Street, London W1V 3HR
USA: 29 West 35th Street, New York, NY 10001–2291

Verso is the imprint of New Left Books

ISBN 0–86091–343–0
ISBN 0–86091–555–7 (Pbk)

British Library Cataloguing in Publication Data
A catalogue record for this book is available from the British Library

Library of Congress Cataloging-in-Publication Data
A catalogue record for this book is available from the Library of Congress

Typeset by Leaper & Gard Ltd, Bristol
Printed in Great Britain by Biddles Ltd.

To E.G.D. and J.E.D.

CONTENTS

PREFACE

Like most works of theory, I suspect, this book is largely auto-biographical. In particular, it represents my attempt to come to terms with two experiences.

I spent about half the 1970s teaching in a London comprehensive school – not very effectively, to be honest. Part of the problem was that although I thought I was starting off on my long march through the institutions, that political arrogance was undermined by the libertarian rhetoric of deschooling, which then passed for educational radicalism. I was haunted by Tolstoy's subversive but ultimately narcissistic question, 'Who has the right to teach?' That issue of educational authority is one of the themes I tackle here. In doing so I have tried to avoid the usual utopian or emancipatory rhetoric. That assumes too easily that education is part of a dialectic of repression and liberation. Posing the question in that way traps you in a vicious loop: inflated promises about both the fulfilment of the child and the development of society are endlessly broken in practice. I began to become critical of such ideas primarily through my studies at Goldsmiths' College and through my involvement in the Society for Education in Film and Television, for whom I later edited the journal *Screen Education*. That eclectic intellectual formation in the new sociology of education and a concern with media texts and institutions shaped by Althusserian Marxism, Lacanian psychoanalysis, semiotics and Brechtian aesthetics, although perhaps not always obvious, no doubt continues to shape the way that here I ask what sort of institution education is. By calling its usual boundaries into question, and by juxtaposing it with the apparatuses and practices of popular culture, I hope to describe its present functions more accurately and suggest some modest democratic possibilities.

The second experience motivating this book was that of working in the field of cultural theory in the 1980s, the era of high Thatcherism. Looking now at courses I worked on at the Open University, like 'Popular Culture' and 'Beliefs and Ideologies', it is clear that their mainly Gramscian orientation reflected a desire to understand the cultural roots, the radical ambition and the social consequences of this curious episode in British political life. Again, the context marks many of these chapters, for they are based on work done then. In revising them, I have tried to emphasize broader explanatory themes, in the hope that these might contribute to the task of dismantling and reconstruction. That the end of my work on the book should have coincided with the soap opera putsch that ousted Mrs Thatcher provided a fortuitous if not unwelcome narrative closure.

In a memorable phrase, Bakhtin described language as being 'populated – overpopulated – with the intentions of others'. Although this is what makes it difficult to seize words as one's own, that resistance is not only a problem. The intimidating business of writing would be impossible if the words and ideas of others were not already in circulation to be appropriated. The connotations of transformation and theft in the idea of appropriation both seem to fit, and my notes and references should be read in that spirit as a catalogue of intellectual debts. To colleagues in the institutions I have mentioned, and those with whom I have worked on the journal *New Formations*, I owe the best part of my education. I must thank Homi Bhabha for his unforgiving generosity in discussing and sharing ideas, and also Paul du Gay and Nancy Wood for their perceptive readings of a full draft of the manuscript. I am grateful for comments on different versions of its various parts, or for conversations about the ideas, to Victor Burgin, Erica Carter, Elizabeth Cowie, Stuart Hall, Geoffrey Hurd, Irene Kotlarz, Gregor McLennan, Colin Mercer, Ali Rattansi, and Valerie Walkerdine.

Some of the chapters draw on material first published in the following: 'Beacons of the Future: Schooling, Subjection and

Subjectification', in Veronica Beechey and James Donald, eds, *Subjectivity and Social Relations*, The Open University and the Open University Press, 1985; 'How English is it? Popular Literature and National Culture', *New Formations*, no. 6, Routledge, 1988; 'Machines of Democracy: Education and Entertainment in Inter-War Britain', *Critical Quarterly*, vol. 30, no. 3, Manchester University Press, 1988; 'The Fantastic, the Sublime and the Popular; Or, What's at Stake in Vampire Films', in James Donald, ed., *Fantasy and the Cinema*, British Film Institute, 1989; 'Interesting Times: Education and Broadcasting in the 1990s', *Critical Social Policy*, no. 27, Critical Social Policy Ltd, 1990.

Illustrations are courtesy of Barnardo's Photographic Library; Columbia/EMI/Warner; Decla-Bioscop; Metropolitan Borough of Stockport, Leisure Services Division, Library of Local Studies Photographic Collection; Orion Pictures; Universal. (Film stills provided by National Film Archive, London, Stills Division.)

INTRODUCTION

Well-Regulated Liberty

In the last text he wrote Freud ruefully acknowledged, as he had on several previous occasions, the limits and frustrations of his work: 'It almost looks as if analysis were the third of those "impossible" professions in which one can be sure beforehand of achieving unsatisfying results. The other two, which have been known much longer, are education and government.' Perhaps he was thinking of an earlier philosopher's perplexity: 'There are two human inventions which may be considered more difficult than any others,' Kant had warned, 'the art of government, and the art of education; and people still contend as to their very meaning.'[1]

This book is a contribution to that perennial contest, another attempt to answer some obvious but still unresolved questions. What sort of institution is education? How is it related to the 'art of government'? Why are they both so difficult not only to do, but even to define? Although I share with Freud and Kant their justified bafflement, this does not lead to a disabling pessimism. On the contrary, it opens up an alternative both to a conservatism which sees all ameliorative political schemes shattering on the rock of the Old Adam, and also to that evangelical radicalism for which education promises not only social justice but also the full expression of human potential. However polarized those positions may be politically, they share a certain logic. Thus is human nature, they say; the problem is to devise social institutions adequate to control it or to realize it. In contrast, to start from the *difficulty* of education and government is to acknowledge that the central enigma is the

1

contingency and the evanescence of both 'human nature' and 'the social'.

Against sociological or psychological narratives about the 'outside' of society impinging on the 'inside' of the individual psyche, I emphasize that the boundaries between the two are never stable or easily enforceable. This involves no choice between the two truisms that 'people make society' and that 'society makes people'. It is true that people act in self-directed and intentional ways, and yet the patterns of consciousness, perception and desire that inform their actions are already aspects of social being. It is equally true that personality is socially determined, and yet people do act in and on social institutions. To unscramble this apparent paradox, I try to show how the field of possible actions is structured and also how these structures are negotiated in practice. The relationship is neither a one-way determination, nor even a dialectic: it is characterized by oscillation, slippage and unpredictable transformations.

My picture of culture is therefore one of a polylogic field of forces. The domain of the social is instituted through the dissemination of intersubjective terms of authority by, for example, the apparatuses of government and education. At the same time, it is in the negotiation, recombination and *bricolage* of these structures that the identification of subjectivity and the individuation of agency emerge contiguously as boundaries. In this approach, identity cannot be derived from a homogeneous notion of collective identity, such as race, class or gender, any more than agency can be attributed to a transcendent individualism. Individuation is achieved in the split between identity and agency, a split which then allows an articulation between the two. To be 'a citizen' in a modern liberal democracy, for example, is to be both a member of the imagined community of the nation *and* a self-conscious and self-monitoring ethical being. But the pedagogic status of the former (its claim to tell you who you are) is always put into doubt by the performativity of the latter (which requires that you be author of your own utterances and actions).[2]

Although subjectivity and agency are effects of these pedagogic norms, then, they are never just their realization. The strategies and discourses of governmental apparatuses tell only half the story. It is equally important to look at the unrecorded but resourceful improvisations of everyday life. Here the cultural norms are transgressed and reworked in the very moment they are instituted. The practices of everyday life, argues Michel de Certeau, 'present themselves essentially as "arts of making" this or that, i.e., as combinatory or utilizing modes of consumption.' It is this performative aspect that he sees as the most important, and often underestimated, characteristic of popular culture. 'These practices bring into play a "popular" *ratio*, a way of thinking invested in a way of acting, an art of combination which cannot be dissociated from an art of using.'[3]

It is to capture the fluidity of the movement in which authoritative norms are enacted and translated in their use that I keep shifting the focus of the discussion in the following chapters between education and popular culture. By refusing to establish a fixed relationship in which one is central and the other marginal, or the one normative and the other subversive, I hope that these shifting points of view might offer new and perhaps unexpected perspectives on the terrain and limits of both domains. They reveal, for example, not only the performative aspects of popular culture, but also the pedagogic functions of national broadcasting systems, Hollywood cinema and popular literature – the cultural industries, in short. The point to stress is that 'popular culture' does not mean just one thing. It refers both to an apparatus that disseminates certain narratives and images, and also to the practices through which these are consumed or rearticulated.

All this activity suggests why the institution and negotiation of cultural authority never produces acquiescence only. The experience of education and the consuming passions of popular culture always generate farce and restlessness and dissonance, as well as pleasure and the aspiration to a general will. In attempting to define limits – between Us and Them, between High and Low – cultural apparatuses also bring into being a constitutive outside, which is represented as the abject, the despised, the obscene, the hybrid and the monstrous. This dark side of modernity is another sign of the impossibility that Freud recognized. The self cannot be perfectly adapted to social norms, even through ever more pervasive techniques of education, government or therapy.

In this Introduction, as a trailer for some of the themes I shall be exploring in more detail later, I look at one example of how the tension between technologies of adaptation and the impossibility of achieving a perfect fit between self and society have been inscribed in post-Enlightenment cultural thought. This is the social imaginary discernible in Rousseau's writings on 'the child' and 'the citizen', and his prescriptions for the forms of education appropriate to them.

Enlightenment and Education

Kant saw education as a way of liberating 'man' from the tutelage and dependence to which ignorance condemned him. This liberty could only be achieved *through* socialization, however, by learning to recover what is natural. 'Man can only become man by education,' he wrote. 'He is merely what education makes him.' To be 'man' is to act freely. But to be able to act freely, to become what he already is in essence, 'man' has to go through a process of socialization, which may be formalized as education or may be the sentimental education of biographical experience. In schooling, Kant insists, the child's capacity for independence and rationality can only be achieved through the imposition of restraint: 'we must prove to him that restraint is only laid upon him that he may learn in time to use his liberty aright, and that his mind is being cultivated so that one day he may be free; that is, independent of the help of others.' Liberty is *managed*. It is a form of conduct to be learned. It is not an Edenic state of absolute freedom beyond the demands and bound-aries of the social, but a capacity for acting autonomously within social rules and forms.[4]

The paradox of individual freedom being achieved through the submission to pedagogic norms is most dramatically expressed by Rousseau. Indeed, at first sight he appears to be saying two quite contradictory things. In *Emile*, he argues passionately that the child needs to be protected from premature exposure to the corruptions of society if it is to have any chance of growing or developing naturally. And yet in *The Social Contract*, he suggests with equal force that it is only through active participation in the business of society that man develops his intellectual and moral capacities:

Although in civil society man surrenders some of the advantages that belong to the state of nature, he gains in return far greater ones; his faculties are so exercised and developed, his sentiments so ennobled, and his whole spirit so elevated that, if the abuse of his new condition did not in many cases lower him to something worse than what he had left, he should constantly bless the happy hour that lifted him for ever from the state of nature and from a stupid, limited animal made a creature of intelligence and a man.

To make sense of this tension, it needs to be plotted against two axes in Rousseau's thought, which intersect in his critique of the liberal social contract as a device for maintaining inequitable social relations. One axis is ethical and teleological. At its retrospective pole, it postulates a state of nature from which a possessive and competitive society emerged, and so indicates the costs as well as the benefits of that transformation. At its prophetic pole, it imagines a future society in which free and equal individuals might create a political order based on self-assumed political obligation – and thus in tune with what is true and enduring in human nature. The axis defined by these poles of a reconstructed 'must-have-been' and a hypothetical 'could-be' makes it possible to chart the weaknesses and duplicities of a corrupt present, as well as the dangers of changes in civil society that do not take account of man's nature. Rousseau's 'return to nature' does not signify regression to primitivism: 'when I want to train a natural man, I do not want to make him a savage and to send him back to the woods.' Rather, it offers a guide to surviving the present and creating a more democratic future. Similarly, the aspiration to freedom suggests not only an imaginable alternative to the experience of alienation, but a critical vantage point from which to deal with it.[5]

Whereas this first axis records social and historical transformations, the other charts the development and growth of the individual. Its poles are defined by Rousseau's contrast between 'the natural man' (or child) and 'the citizen': 'The natural man lives for himself; he is the unit, the whole, dependent only on himself and his like. The citizen is but the numerator of a fraction, whose value depends on the community.' Rousseau recommends Plato's *Republic* as a guide to the education of citizens: children would have to be taken from their parents at birth and reared collectively. 'Good social institutions are those best fitted to make a man unnatural, to exchange his independence for dependence, to merge the unit in the group, so that he no longer regards himself as one but as part of the whole, and is only conscious of the common life.' *Emile*, by contrast, tells us how children should be educated in order to remain – or become – natural. Whereas citizens must be educated against nature, in accordance with the demands of society, boys and girls should be educated against society, in accordance with the innate pattern of their psychological development and their physical maturation.[6]

This is the *nature* of children, which needs to be isolated from harmful social influences: 'Their defects of mind and body may all be traced to the same source, the desire to make men of them before their time.' But this nature cannot simply be allowed free rein: 'there are so many contradictions between the rights of nature and the laws of society that to conciliate them we must continually contradict ourselves. Much art is required to prevent man in society from being altogether artificial.' Here the role of the Tutor becomes crucial in managing the child's environment in order to provoke the spontaneous but desired changes:

> Let [your pupil] always think he is master while you are really master. There is no subjection so complete as that which preserves the forms of freedom; it is thus that the will itself is taken captive. Is not this poor child, without knowledge, strength, or wisdom, entirely at your mercy? Are you not master of his whole environment so far as it affects him? Cannot you make of him what you please? His work and play, his pleasure and pain, are they not, unknown to him, under your control? No doubt he ought only to do what he wants, but he ought to want to do nothing but what you want him to do.

The education Rousseau recommends thus involves the artifice and manipulation of 'well-regulated liberty' rather than coercion or instruction. This regulation requires the definition of an external authority to which the child/citizen is subject, and yet which authorizes him to act as a free agent. In *Emile*, this authority is that of nature; in *The Social Contract* that of the general will. In both cases, the capacities and rules that enable the subject to know, to speak and to act are dramatized in a figure whose mastery and disinterested love are displayed through an incontrovertible competence: the Tutor and the Lawgiver. These then provide a point of symbolic identification: that is, 'identification with the very place *from where* we are being observed, *from where* we look at ourselves so that we appear to ourselves likeable, worthy of love.' It is thus as Emile identifies with the authoritative position from which he is observed by the Tutor that he is given a mandate to act as a free agent within the intersubjective symbolic network.[7]

In *Emile*, this agency appears as the interiorization of a second nature that seeks to recreate the virtue embodied in the state of nature: a state deduced from man's potential for perfectibility within society. As Ernst Cassirer noted, Rousseau 'requires that Emile be educated *outside* society, because in this way alone can he be educated *for* society in the only true sense.' Thus the production of the good citizen comes to be understood as the supposed liberation of the natural child. If 'man was born free, and he is everywhere in chains', the future freedom to which Rousseau aspires is the transformation of these mind-forg'd manacles into equitable and reciprocal commitments between society and individual, into intersubjective bonds of union and love and respect. The virtuous citizen is the one who experiences these bonds as his or her own desires, aspirations and guilt, and thus evinces the capacity for self-policing. The well-ordered modern polity is one that depends less on coercion than on this self-policing of free citizens, and so can claim the authority of virtue and nature.[8]

Youth, Nature and Virtue

Rousseau's stories about the socialization of youth and the formation of citizens did not just have a profound influence on educators like Pestalozzi in Europe and Horace Mann in the United States. They also set in place a definitive narrative of what it is to be, and to become, a social actor. This version of sentimental education was to be widely elaborated, amended and contested in works of fiction and philosophy.

7

Emile, published in 1762, can thus be seen as paving the way for the *Bildungsroman* tradition in the European novel, with its tales of the moral formation of young men (or less often women) as they move from a restrictive provincial society to the dynamic but unsettling context of the city. The founding text of this tradition, Goethe's *The Years of Apprenticeship of Wilhelm Meister* (1795–1806), takes from Rousseau not only his reconceptualized category of youth, but also the imagery of 'storm and stress', which fleshes out his view of the disjuncture between the growth of individual capacities and desires and social codes of behaviour. What Wilhelm Meister learns in his biographical tribulations is to make choices that weigh the *authenticity* of the self against the demands of *convention*.[9] This *Bildungsroman* narrative not only reflected a new experience of learning to live with uncertainty and vulnerability, and even learning to transform them into a capacity for self-creation and recreation; it also disseminated the categories of authenticity and convention, self and society, and creativity and compulsion, which produced the terms for a new mode of conduct, a new relation of the self to the self.

It was around these newly constituted oppositions that the *Bildungsroman* split into two major strands. The more conservative novels stress the degree of success in the adaptation of the self to social norms, the comforts of civilization, and so also the price of modernity represented by the loss of stability, authority and community. Formally, these novels tend to emphasize narrative closure. Often, the achievement of social integration and the resolution of the plot are figured as a marriage, preferrably one uniting aristocracy and bourgeoisie. In Elizabeth Bennett's marriage to Darcy in Jane Austen's *Pride and Prejudice*, for example, the terms of a social contract are clearly translated into bonds of mutual love and obligation. The more radical and romantic novels – those by Stendhal and Pushkin, for example, or the strand that runs from Balzac to Flaubert – value the possibility of personal change and transformation at the expense of the demands of the social. They celebrate youth over maturity, experiment over stability, freedom over happiness. Instead of pulling all the events of a story into the frame imposed by an ending, they dismiss the possibility of a closure (narrative or social) that will resolve all tensions and ambiguities.

The split over the fragility and costs of social order suggests why adultery recurs as a motif in both strands: a novel like *Madame Bovary* explores the transgression of contractual relations and the pain of either virtuous conformity or delinquent desire.[10]

It was primarily Romantic philosophers who took up the *Bildungsroman*'s categorical opposition between authenticity and normality in their attempt to identify the capacities and competences necessary for self-formation. One of these was the practice of aesthetic reflection, and it was in this context that 'literature' and 'culture' were set in place as authoritative pedagogic categories. In *On the Aesthetic Education of Man*, for example – published, like Goethe's *Wilhelm Meister*, in 1795 – Schiller reconceptualized Rousseau's distinction between *l'homme naturel* and *l'homme artificiel*, not in terms of fall and redemption, but more sociologically as a breach produced within man's ethical substance by the division of labour and the differentiation of spheres. But although 'it was civilization [*Kultur*] itself which inflicted this wound upon modern man', it was nevertheless only culture that could heal the split between man's sensuous and rational drives. For Schiller, it is the task of culture 'to do justice to both drives equally: not simply to maintain the rational against the sensuous, but the sensuous against the rational too'. Works of art and literature could mediate and transcend the two drives through the impulse to *play* – a play regulated by the aesthetic tradition in much the same way as Emile's tutor had managed the boy's physical environment. Thus the cultural authority of the Tutor was embodied in the works of art themselves. If studied properly, they demand, and so inculcate, perception, discrimination and self-correction. Although the development of such attributes does not represent a return to nature in Rousseau's sense, it too aspires to a state in which the dissociation of sensibility produced by the social is healed – here through the harmonizing techniques of aesthetic response.[11]

At the same time as Goethe and Schiller were extending Rousseau's ideas about youth, education and self-formation, others were subjecting them to more subversive readings. In her *Vindication of the Rights of Woman* (1792), for example, Mary Wollstonecraft had to recast Rousseau's account of socialization and citizenship in her attempt to rescue his republicanism for feminism. The scale and difficulty of the project is made evident by Rousseau's account of Sophy as the ideal companion for Emile. 'Sophy should be as truly a woman as Emile is a man, i.e., she must possess all those characters of her sex which are required to enable her to play her part in the physical and moral order.' That role, woman's nature, is a docile servility, which disbars her from participation in the political life of the community. Her education should be guided by the fact that 'woman is made to please and to be in subjection to man':

> To be pleasing in his sight, to win his respect and love, to train him in childhood, to tend him in manhood, to counsel and console, to make his life pleasant and happy, these are the duties of woman for all time, and this is what she should be taught while she is young.

Whereas Rousseau here invokes the brute fact of nature to justify women's exclusion from public participation, Wollstonecraft attributes sexual difference to the crippling conventions of socialization. If women become little more than 'insignificant objects of desire', then blame their upbringing; if they become 'rakes at heart', then that is 'the inevitable consequence of their education'. 'Considering the length of time the women have been dependent,' asks Wollstonecraft, 'is it surprising that some of them hug their chains, and fawn like the spaniel?' For her, it was the unjustified and unjust 'divine right of husbands', not any natural deficiency, that disabled women. Women shared with men the God-given capacity to reason, even if this had atrophied through lack of use. If Rousseau's misrecognition of cultural attributes as innate characteristics were corrected, bourgeois women would become citizens as virtuous, effective and revolutionary as any man.[12]

Wollstonecraft goes beyond Rousseau by stressing that the exercise of liberty is contingent on having the means and opportunities to pursue self-chosen ends as well as to fulfil social obligations. Although she ascribes the degenerate state of women to culture rather than nature, however, she neither disputes Rousseau's assessment of the potential danger to social order of untrammelled female desire nor challenges his categories of nature and culture. The argument is once again that corruption should be ascribed to the effects of society, and that (women's) nature is inherently virtuous and rational. Wollstonecraft reproduces the Enlightenment view of liberty through socialization: woman can only become woman by education.

A more spectacularly transgressive version of this argument appeared in the same post-Revolutionary moment as Wollstone-craft's *Vindication*. Whereas she tried to recuperate Rousseau's ideas, the Marquis de Sade's *Philosophy in the Bedroom* (1795) challenged their very foundations. Not only does Sade revel in the poly-morphousness and irrationality of human desires, pleasures, per-versions and cruelties, he also vigorously reviles the self-deception and hypocrisy of those virtuous citizens who disavow them. Here, then, is another tutor addressing his charge – this time Sade's Dolmancé:

> Ah, Eugénie, have done with virtues! Among the sacrifices that can be made to these counterfeit divinities is there one worth an instant of the pleasures one tastes in outraging them? Come, my sweet, virtue is but a chimera whose worship consists exclusively in perpetual immolations, in unnumbered rebellions against the temperament's inspirations. Can such impulses be natural? Does Nature recommend what offends her? Eugénie, be not the dupe of those women you hear called virtuous. Theirs are not, if you wish, the same passions as ours; but they hearken to others, and often more contemptible. ... There is ambition, there pride, there you find self-seeking ...[13]

Eugénie, it has been suggested, is the double of the modest Sophy. Her transgressions are not only a deliberate affront to Sophy's virtues – as in the viciously ingenious vengeance she wreaks on her mother, the embodiment of long-suffering Rousseauian femininity – but also help to define their scope and limits. Virtue, proclaims Sade, cannot be rooted in nature because nature is radically amoral. This is the heresy, as William Connolly observes, that explodes Rousseau's moral universe.

> The Sadeian storm of passion and cruelty, raging within four walls of an imaginary bedroom, underlines the cosmic proportions of his oppo-nents' narcissistic delusions: they demand that God inscribe guidelines and protections for the human comedy in the text of nature; they insist that the design of nature itself revolve around the fate of humanity![14]

11

Sade thus de-deifies Nature, and by extension Reason too, in so far as that is seen as an innate human capacity. He recasts the repression, self-deception and alienation imposed on the self by the demands of a socially prescribed virtue in terms more violently compelling than the *Bildungsroman* authors or the Romantic philosophers dared to consider. When he sketches his own version of the good society in the 'anonymous' pamphlet incorporated into *Philosophy in the Bedroom*, it is radically opposed to Rousseau's austere and strenuous republicanism. 'Yet Another Effort, Frenchmen, If You Would Become Republicans' envisages a minimal state that would set the stage for a libidinal anarchy.

Government

Of course, Sade's account of nature, desire and agency, and the movement between them, is no more definitive than Rousseau's or Wollstonecraft's. By putting the normative categories and narratives of Enlightenment education so profoundly in question, however, Sade's pornographic pedagogy provides a useful contrast against which to set the techniques of public and mass schooling, which emerged in the nineteenth and twentieth centuries. These have persistently attempted to shape children to their measure by means of disciplines that claim, like Rousseau's Tutor and Sade's Dolmancé, not only to understand the nature of the child, but to be able to emancipate it. They follow Rousseau rather than Sade, however, in suggesting that this will recover for civil society the virtues of its uncorrupted state. And they have followed the Romantic philosophers by proposing techniques of self-formation and self-monitoring based on self-expression within a morally managed environment.

In this light, schooling can be seen as the paradigm of modern techniques of government. It works by deploying an intimate knowledge of the individuals who make up its target population, and an expertise in monitoring and guiding their conduct. Nikolas Rose explains this *pastoral* exercise of power in *Governing the Soul*:

The conceptual systems devised within the 'human' sciences, the languages of analysis and explanation that they invented, the ways of speaking about human conduct that they constituted, have provided the means whereby human subjectivity and intersubjectivity could enter the calculations of the authorities. On the one hand, subjective features of human life can become elements within understandings of the economy, the organization, the prison, the school, the factory and the labour market. On the other, the human psyche itself has become a possible domain for systematic government in the pursuit of socio-political ends. Educate, cure, reform, punish – these are old imperatives no doubt. But the new vocabularies provided by the sciences of the psyche enable the aspirations of government to be articulated in terms of the knowledgeable management of the depths of the human soul.[15]

This sceptical attitude to the politics of expertise makes clear the logic of progressive education. The Plowden Report of 1967, for example, enshrines a powerful and influential justification of a 'child-centred' approach to primary schooling. On page 1 it proclaims the Rousseauian axiom that 'underlying all educational questions is the nature of the child himself'. Now, however, know-ledge about 'the nature of the child' has been formalized as a scien-tific discipline: the developmental psychology associated especially with the work of Jean Piaget. This identifies a supposedly natural pattern of maturation and growth that should guide teachers in their decisions about what, how and when to teach their pupils. In prac-tice, however, it can equally well be read as a normative grid for the observation and classification of children. 'Allowing the child to develop' has instituted an emphasis on surveillance and monitoring; 'liberating the child' has involved stratagems as lovingly manipula-tive as any of those devised by Emile's tutor.[16]

The paradox remains, however, that a degree of autonomous agency is a precondition of pastoral modes of power. Far from negating or denying freedom, argues Foucault, power requires freedom:

> Power is exercised only over free subjects, and only in so far as they are free. By this we mean individual or collective subjects who are faced with a field of possibilities in which several ways of behaving, several reactions and diverse comportments may be realized. Where the deter-mining factors saturate the whole there is no relationship of power ...

This conception of power defines the conditions in which Foucault's 'governmentality' becomes a possibility. Here the subject is not only *subject to* the play of forces in the apparatuses of the social, but must also act as author and *subject of* its own conduct. This ambivalent freedom – never absolute heteronomy nor pure autonomy – is necessary because the machinery of government can only work on agency:

> 'Government' ... designated the way in which the conduct of individuals or of groups might be directed: the government of children, of souls, of communities, of families, of the sick. It did not only cover the legitimately constituted forms of political or economic subjection, but also modes of action, more or less considered and calculated, which were destined to act upon the possibilities of action of other people. To govern, in this sense, is to structure the possible field of action of others.

Freedom thus appears not as the innate characteristic of a transcendent individual, but as the negotiation that produces individuation. Foucault calls it an *agonism*: 'a relationship which is at the same time reciprocal incitation and struggle; less of a face-to-face confrontation which paralyses both sides than a permanent provocation.'[17]

This freedom is a reminder that authority is always open to question, that reason is inescapably agonistic and recursive. It entails a scepticism towards foundational or expressive categories and a critical reflection on the institution and negotiation of authority. That is why I am suspicious of educational programmes designed to 'develop people's creative potential', or political schemes that promise to create 'the conditions for the full realization of human talents'.[18] Such claims not only disavow the impossibility of education and government; in doing so, they also cede to the pedagogues or the philosophers or the party leaders the authority to define what human nature is, and so allow them to pre-empt the necessary dialogue about (for example) the purposes of education in a democracy.

Instead of chasing the dangerous Enlightenment dream of universal virtue, it would make more sense to revive the republican emphasis on participation, autonomy and civic obligations – but recasting them in the knowledge that they can only take effect as they move through popular culture, as they are wilfully and often perversely enacted in the inventive arts of everyday life. My aim is therefore to question the existing boundaries of education, and to ask how certain narratives and categories are instituted as authoritative. In asking who has authority over education, for example, I would not take the conventional actors of liberal politics – parents, children, employers, parties, classes, governments – at face value. Rather, I would question how the staging of political dialogue produces these categories as collective actors with common interests: that is, how the terrain of educational debate is constantly made and remade. The disjunctive liminality of this negotiation is well expressed in Homi Bhabha's description of the contested territory in which the 'double-time' of the people is played out:

> The people are the historical 'objects' of a nationalist pedagogy, giving the discourse an authority that is based on the pre-given or constituted historical origin or event; the people are also the 'subjects' of a process of signification that must erase any prior or originary presence of the nation-people to demonstrate the prodigious, living principle of the people as that continual process by which the national life is redeemed and signified as a repeating and reproductive process.[19]

It is because these two rhythms are never quite in time with each other that the boundaries between education, government and popular culture are never settled. Sometimes the pedagogic and the popular coincide, sometimes they overlap and sometimes they are in conflict.

This is not to forgo conventional politics, but rather to acknowledge its specificity and the necessarily provisional or particularistic status of its discourse. Bhabha's account of the articulation between the pedagogic and the performative also shifts the focus away from an exclusive concern with this delimited sphere and onto the everyday, the normal and the routine as a locus of analysis and intervention. It is here, in today's lesson or in watching the television tonight, that the singular dramas of authority and agency are played out.

These are stories not just about reason and intentionality, but

especially about the messy dynamics of desire, fantasy and transgression. I am dealing with forms of living that are, to quote Homi
Bhabha again,

> more complex than 'community'; more symbolic than 'society'; ...
> more rhetorical than the reason of state; more mythological than
> ideology; less homogeneous than hegemony; less centred than the
> citizen; more collective than 'the subject'; more psychic than civility;
> more hybrid in the articulation of cultural differences and identifica-
> tions – gender, race or class – than can be represented in any hier-
> archical or binary structuring of social antagonism.[20]

It is this instability and mobility – this impossibility – that I
explore in what follows. In Chapter 1, I examine the pedagogic
techniques and structures of authority instituted in English popular
education in the nineteenth century. In the first part of Chapter 2, I
continue this argument by considering the *symbolic* authority
invested in the category Literature in relation to the formation of
national cultures. In the second part, I tackle the relationship
between Literature and 'the nation' from a different angle, through
an argument about popular fiction and popular reading. Chapter 3
traces the formation of a certain conception of national culture in
response to the perceived threats of mass politics and mass society in
Britain between the world wars. Chapter 4 is a brief theoretical
interlude, which spells out some points of difference between my
approach and that of other writers with whom I share a broadly
post-Foucauldian orientation.[21] In Chapter 5, I approach the
instability of symbolic boundaries through the genre of the fantastic,
the aesthetic and philosophical category of the sublime, and the
sociological and political category of the popular. This leads to a
reformulated idea of community, which sets the scene for the more
topical and political concerns of Chapters 6 and 7. These look at
recent developments in broadcasting and education, and suggest
some possibilities for change.

1

BEACONS OF THE FUTURE

The State as Educator

In Arthur Conan Doyle's 'The Naval Treaty', first published in the
Strand magazine in 1893, Sherlock Holmes and Dr Watson are on a
train heading back to London from a case in the Home Counties:

> Holmes was sunk in profound thought and hardly opened his mouth
> until we had passed Clapham Junction.
>
> 'It's a very cheery thing to come into London by any of these lines
> which run high and allow you to look down upon the houses like this.'
>
> I thought he was joking, for the view was sordid enough, but he soon
> explained himself.
>
> 'Look at those big, isolated clumps of buildings arising up above the
> slates, like brick islands in a lead-coloured sea.'
>
> 'The board-schools.'
>
> 'Light-houses, my boy! Beacons of the future! Capsules with
> hundreds of little seeds in each, out of which will spring the wiser, better
> England of the future. I suppose that man Phelps does not drink?'

What were these board schools that so captured the imagination
of the usually cynical detective? They had been established only a
couple of decades earlier, in 1870, by the Elementary Education Act
introduced by W.E. Forster during Gladstone's first Liberal administration. Their express purpose was to extend education for the
working-class children by 'filling the gaps' in the schooling already
provided by a number of religious societies. They were administered
by locally elected school boards, which had, for the first time, the
power to levy a rate for education. Attendance did not finally
become compulsory until 1880. Nor were the schools free; it was

only in 1891 that boards were given the discretion to do away with the 'school pence'. In short, the board schools introduced universal, state-funded, compulsory elementary education to England.

For Holmes, though, they seem to represent something more. The schools are not just 'clumps of buildings'. They are 'brick islands', recognizable and reassuring landmarks breaking up potentially dangerous enclaves as they rise out of the 'lead-coloured sea' of working-class London. Nor is it just physically that they open out these apparently impenetrable areas. As 'light-houses' they bring moral illumination into the proletarian murk. As 'beacons of the future', they are catalysts of a political and ethical evolution towards 'the wiser, better England of the future'.

How was it that this utopian vision could appear, in a popular fiction in 1893, as no more than common sense? What had been happening in debates about education and in the provision of schooling over previous decades to make this imagery possible? To grasp the changing social and cultural dynamics involved, it will be necessary to view the history from three different angles, to follow three lines of investigation.

The first focuses on educational ideologies as such – the beliefs, values, grievances and aspirations articulated around the term 'education', and to be found in government reports, parliamentary debates, journalism, treatises on pedagogy and even popular detective fiction. It was during the nineteenth century that 'education' took on its metaphoric currency in political debate, and a profusion of schemes bear witness to competing visions of how best to school children (however perceived) in order to achieve the good society (however imagined): from the Anglican Dr Bell's 'Madras system' for the efficient indoctrination of religious and patriotic beliefs among the poor in the first decades of the century to the communitarian socialist schooling provided by Robert Owen at New Lanark; from the attempts to create a rational, secular society by Chartist autodidacts like William Lovett to the elitist social engineering of public school advocates like Dr Arnold; from the anti-reformist Robert Lowe's reluctant acknowledgement that the extension of the franchise in the 1860s meant that 'it will be absolutely necessary to compel our future masters to learn their letters' to the Fabian Sydney Webb's meritocratic vision at the turn of the twentieth century of an educational ladder enabling clever children to escape from the working class.

My second line of inquiry is to see how the human sciences were deployed in the emerging routines of schooling – theories of child development, for example, or changing pedagogic techniques. Here we are dealing less with political language than with the operations of power and knowledge, power through knowledge. Like Foucault, I am interested in the 'subtle mechanisms' through which power is exercised, and which 'cannot but evolve, organize and put into circulation a knowledge, or rather apparatuses of knowledge, which are not ideological constructs'.[1]

The target of these mechanisms was primarily 'the individual', a category they help to bring into effective being. Their objective was the inculcation of certain social norms as personal attributes. *Self-monitoring* is the key to Foucault's conception of panopticism. That is not quite the same as saying that we live in the iron cage of a totally administered society. Foucault unpicks the variety of practices that make a particular type of experience historically possible, and then offers a consciously anti-ideological explanation of how the process works. Here I take a different approach, arguing that the dynamics of the symbolic are essential to the ascription of ethical dispositions as personal desires.[2] The unconscious is not as biddable as the Foucauldian model sometimes implies, nor desire so malleable. My third line of inquiry will therefore be to examine why knowledge is organized in the particular form of the school curriculum, and what subjective dispositions this might produce.

Schools for the People

Apart from workhouse schools for the children of paupers, it was not until the 1830s that the English state became formally, and grudgingly, involved in the provision of schooling for working-class children. Since the beginning of the century, there had been pressure for such provision, not least from people alarmed by the spectre of a literate and radical working class summoned up by the massive popular response to Tom Paine's *Rights of Man*. In 1807, the liberal Whig leader Samuel Whitbread introduced a Bill in the

House of Commons for establishing parish schools. Although it was the opposition of the Lords that finally defeated it, the tenor of the traditionalist objection to the diffusion of popular education was best captured in the notorious speech by Davies Giddy, the President of the Royal Society:

> However specious in theory the project might be of giving education to the labouring classes of the poor, it would, in effect, be found prejudicial to their morals and happiness, it would teach them to despise their lot in life, instead of making them good servants in agriculture, and other laborious employments to which their rank in society had destined them; instead of teaching them subordination, it would render them factious and refractory, as was evident in the manufacturing counties; it would enable them to read seditious pamphlets, vicious books, and publications against Christianity; it would render them insolent to their superiors; and in a few years, the result would be, that the legislators would find it necessary to direct the strong arm of power against them, and to furnish the executive magistrates with more vigorous powers than were now in force. Besides, if the bill were to pass into law, it would go to burthen the country with a most enormous and incalculable expense, and to load the industrious orders with still heavier imposts.

Whereas Giddy feared its potential subversiveness, more far-sighted Tory thinkers realized that popular education might in the long run provide a more pervasive and thus stronger 'arm of power' than crude repression by the magistrates.

Patrick Colquhoun was himself a London magistrate, but he was also one of the first social investigators to pose the question of how effectively to govern an industrial and increasingly urban proletariat. He amassed often lurid statistics to demonstrate the extent and gravity of the problems posed by the 'labouring classes' – including novel correlations between illiteracy and criminality – and lobbied energetically for an organized police force. But his vision of policing was an expansive one, which included a concern with the general health, welfare, recreations and sentiments of the population. The aim was to ensure the strength of the state *through* the improvement of the life of the citizen. It is no surprise, therefore, to find him, in 1806, setting out his ideas for a *New and Appropriate System of Education for the Labouring People*:

the higher and noble aim of preventing those calamities which led to idleness and crime, and produce poverty and misery, by guiding and properly directing the early conduct of the lower orders of the community, and by giving a right bias to their minds, has not, as yet, generally attracted the notice of those who move in the more elevated walks of society.... The prosperity of every state depends on the good habits, and the religious and moral instruction of the labouring people. By shielding the minds of youth against the vices that are most likely to beset them, much is gained to society in the prevention of crimes, and in lessening the demand for punishments.... It is not, however, proposed by this institution, that the children of the poor should be educated in a manner to elevate their minds above the rank they are destined to fill in society, or that an expense should be incurred beyond the lowest rate ever paid for instruction. Utopian schemes for an extensive diffusion of knowledge would be injurious and absurd.

What is new here is not a radically different political perspective from Giddy's: both want to protect the social hierarchy and both are good Tories in not wanting to spend too much money in doing so. It is Colquhoun's way of posing the problem that opens up the possibility of new techniques of government.

At this stage, these did not necessarily entail the involvement of the state. The institution of which Colquhoun had such high hopes was the monitorial school developed by the Anglican Dr Andrew Bell – initially in the context of colonial India. Colquhoun was the chairman of the Committee for Bell's Free School in Orange Street, Westminster. Here the youngest pupils were to be taught by their elders acting as tutors, with an elite of the eldest being appointed monitors, themselves responsible to the master or mistress who sat spider-like at the centre of this web. Colquhoun described how this regime of surveillance, inspection and regulation was supposed to operate:

> The province of the master or mistress is to direct the whole machine in all its parts.... It is their business to see that others work, rather than work themselves. The master and mistress, from their respective chairs, overlook every part of the school, and give life and motion to the whole. They inspect the classes [the children sitting in one row] one after another; call upon the monitors occasionally to bring them up, that they may specifically examine the progress of each pupil.

However elegant the panoptic logic of the scheme, most of the schools set up by Dr Bell's National Society and his nonconformist rival Dr Lancaster's British and Foreign School Society proved neither effective nor popular. What they taught was limited to the most basic instruction in literacy, computation and morality. The nonconformists were more restrained in their religious indoctrination and more expansive in their conception of literacy, including in it a limited degree of writing. This was in line with the Methodist conception of personal responsibility for interpreting the Scriptures as a guide to conduct, but it was anathema to the Anglican Evangelicals. The energetic ideologist and pamphleteer Hannah More had long been active in popular education, having set up Sunday Schools in the Mendip area in the late 1790s: 'I allow of no writing for the poor,' she protested when criticized by some of her Tory allies. 'My object is not to make them fanatics, but to train up the lower classes in habits of industry and piety.' Whatever the intentions, the London showcases of the rival factions, themselves far from perfect, remained atypical. The radical journalist William Cobbett was probably justified in condemning the dismal reality of this 'Bell and Lancaster work' as 'heddekashun', an imposed and deadening form of discipline and instruction.

Nevertheless, when the social tremors caused by the 1832 Reform Act and the waxing of Chartism as a coherent political programme in the 1830s gave the question of how to manage the population a new urgency, the first steps were taken to bring these schools within the ambit of the state. In 1833, Parliament tentatively voted funds of around £20,000 to be paid in unconditional grants to the two voluntary societies; and in 1839 the Committee of the Privy Council on Education was set up, with Sir James Kay-Shuttleworth as its Secretary, to administer the grants and to introduce a system of inspection along the lines laid down in the factory legislation of the time. Underlying both the regulation of work and the socialization of youth was the strategy of policing the working classes – in the sense of monitoring and catering for their welfare. One of the early factory inspectors, Leonard Horner, wrote in a letter in 1837:

> To put the necessity of properly educating the children of the working classes on its lowest footing, it is loudly called for as a matter of police, to

prevent a multitude of immoral and vicious beings, the offspring of ignorance, from growing up around us, to be a pest and a nuisance to society; it is necessary in order to render the great body of the working class governable by reason.

For Kay-Shuttleworth, rendering the working class governable by reason required the inculcation of reason in the working class. Although happy to express this vision in conventional denunciations of 'men so ignorant and so unprincipled as the Chartist leaders' and the need for education in order to 'promote the security of property and the maintenance of public order', he actually perceived the landscape of the social through the same 'bio-political' grid that Colquhoun had earlier mapped out in his *Treatise on the Police of the Metropolis*. Rather than defining the 'dangerous classes' in terms of innate pauperism and criminality, however, Kay-Shuttleworth presents them as the pathological victims of environmental factors. This *moral environmentalism* characterized the first phase of social intervention by the state roughly from 1839 to 1860. It was a primarily medical paradigm of 'the social question' – like many of the new Benthamite state administrators Kay-Shuttleworth had been a doctor – that itself constituted a new technique for regulating the population. To pre-empt the dangers of moral and social corruption as well as contagion, these professional reformers proposed programmes for social hygiene, breaking up the dense working-class enclaves created by industrialization and urbanization. Collecting detailed information about the lives of their inhabitants was to be the prelude to improving their welfare and so civilizing their morals.[3]

This strategy created its own genre of writing. Kay-Shuttleworth's *The Moral and Physical Condition of the Working Classes Employed in the Cotton Manufactures in Manchester* (1832) is an early example of the social explorer's investigations into dangerous and mysterious quarters. Like its successors, from Engels to Mayhew and Booth, it is presented as a nightmare journey to the centre of corruption:

He whose duty is to follow in the steps of this messenger of death [cholera] must descend to the abodes of poverty, must frequent the close alleys, the crowded courts ... and behold with alarm, in the hot bed of pestilence, ills that fester in secret at the very heart of society.

From this starting point of 'ills' and 'pestilence' he spins out a chain of imagery linking susceptibility to contagion among the poor with criminality, moral and physical depravity, and political sedition. Against this, Kay-Shuttleworth (a founder-member of the Manchester Statistical Society) counterposes his social scientific, corrective mode of investigation:

> In Manchester, Boards of Health were established, in each of the fourteen districts of Police, for the purpose of minutely inspecting the state of the houses and streets. These districts were divided into minute sections, to each of which two or more inspectors were appointed from among the most respectable inhabitants of the vicinity, and they were provided with tabular queries, applying to each particular house and street.

What emerges from the interweaving of these two strands is a particular representation of the working-class family, and especially the child, as dangerous primarily because itself *in danger*. The family and the child are thus set in place as the object, mechanism and justification of state intervention.[4]

The supposed benefits of this mix of control and welfare provision were the substance of the case for involving the state in popular education. In trying to put such programmes into practice, however, reformers like Kay-Shuttleworth ran into the resistance not only of political opponents but of the machinery of government itself.

One result of central government's increasing financial involvement in education, however marginal, was that its funding became increasingly subject to the rules and conflicts governing the budgeting of public expenditure. (By the time Kay-Shuttleworth retired in 1849, the yearly grant to the Committee of Council had increased sixfold to £125,000 and within another decade, by 1858, the newly established Science and Art Department was disbursing over £663,000.) Along with this increased expenditure went increasing monitoring of the recipients' activities, and during this time the inspection initiated by Kay-Shuttleworth to ensure minimum standards, although still limited, was made more systematic and rigorous.

The 1850s and 1860s also saw an unprecedented series of Royal

Commissions investigating aspects of educational provision, especially for the children of the bourgeoisie in the universities of Oxford and Cambridge, the public schools (Clarendon) and the endowed schools (Taunton). The only one of the Royal Commissions not to result in major legislation was the Newcastle Report on the elementary schools. This had been charged to 'enquire into the present State of Popular Education in England, and to consider and report what measures, if any, are required for the Extension of sound and cheap elementary instruction to all classes of the People'. The Commission's support for the idea of a county rate for education (while leaving the voluntary system intact) was not taken up. Its proposals that teachers' salaries should be made partly dependent on children's results was greeted more warmly by politicians, who shared the generally low opinion of teachers and who were committed to cutting public expenditure.

The technique for implementing this system of 'payment by results' was the Revised Code, introduced in 1862 by Robert Lowe, then Secretary of the Education Department, and finally put into operation in 1863. This led to a decrease in the level of grant disbursal (from £800,000 in 1861 to £600,000 in 1865), an increased degree of central inspection and control and a curriculum restricted even more tightly to rote learning and the '3 Rs'. 'I cannot promise the House that this system will be an economical one,' Lowe told the Commons, 'and I cannot promise that it will be an efficient one, but I can promise that it shall be one or the other. If it is not cheap, it shall be efficient; if it is not efficient it shall be cheap.'

Lowe simply did not accept (at this stage) the premises of a bio-political strategy. Taking a more *laissez-faire* view of government, he remained sceptical about the power of education to ensure either the welfare or discipline of the population. In taking this position, he provoked the hostility not only of Kay-Shuttleworth, who in his retirement continued to advocate education as the necessary corollary of democracy, but also of Anglican bishops like 'Soapy Sam' Wilberforce; nonconformist clerics, who feared the Code might be the prelude to the withdrawal of funding for their schools; and school inspectors like Matthew Arnold, who bemoaned the increased reliance on the 'mechanical examination'. The Revised Code, in short, highlighted a problem within the bio-political strategy. As responsibility for the provision of welfare assistance shifted from philanthropic to state agencies, so its actual costs as well as its potential social benefits came into the calculation. The problem was exacerbated because promises that education and schemes of social hygiene would reduce crime and pauperism in the cities were not fulfilled.

In the period leading up to Forster's 1870 Education Act, however, several factors combined to build up the pressure for change. New manufacturing technologies, growing challenges to England's industrial supremacy, transitions in the forms of working-class radicalism and the extension of the adult male suffrage by the second Reform Act of 1867, the emergence of increasingly mass-oriented cultural industries: all these, combined with the glaring inadequacies of the existing voluntary schools, meant that the principle of state-provided elementary education became more generally accepted.

The limitations of moral environmentalism, as well as this changed political and economic context, led to new formulations of the social question from the 1860s onwards. The danger now identified was the possible deterioration in the quality of the population; increasingly, however, the focus of attention shifted from the social and moral environment of the population to the inherent aptitudes and/or inadequacies of the individual. Such fears again placed the population question explicitly on the political agenda.[5]

In terms of the individual, concern focused on mental deficiency and degeneracy; this was given a scientific footing through the psychologist Francis Galton's assertions about the inheritability of intelligence. In terms of the population, especially the urban population during the so-called 'Great Depression' of the 1870s, 1880s and 1890s, attention was directed to a newly identified social grouping with specific characteristics: the unemployed and/or the unemployable. Charles Booth's *Life and Labour of the People of London* (1897) attributes their status less to natural viciousness than to a process of urban degeneration. The residuum is seen as susceptible to all those forms of vice that flourish in the margins of metropolitan life – vagrancy, crime, alcoholism, prostitution – and feed on the defects in character of the unemployable individual. These are supposed to explain not only such physical manifestations as poor eyesight, bad hearing, small size, scrofula, phthisis, sterility, but also the mental defects of cretinism and insanity. (It is impossible not to hear in Booth's catalogues echoes of another key text for understanding popular fears about degeneracy, also published in 1897. Bram Stoker's *Dracula* differs from earlier vampire tales by insisting that the terror is 'nineteenth century up-to-date with a vengeance'. Although it reassuringly displaces the original vampirism onto the foreign count, the novel ambivalently pictures an invasive evil penetrating and spreading through the native population once a single person has been corrupted.)[6]

One corollary of these anxieties about the 'fitness' of the population during the last decades of the century was the aspiration to breed – and educate – an 'imperial race'. As the military humiliation of the Boer War coincided with increased industrial competition from Germany, America and Japan, it became clear that the stupefying routines of schooling under the Revised Code were inadequate to the task. The watchword now became National Efficiency, a programme for redefining and extending the powers of the state through reforms in government, industry and social organization, as well as education. Campaigns were launched for a broader curriculum in the elementary schools, which would not only beat the nationalist drum through newly established subjects like history and geography, but would also provide training for citizenship through systematic instruction in social duty or lessons in civics, physical exercise and military-style drill for boys, and instruction in the responsibilities and techniques of domesticity and motherhood for girls.[7]

This concern with the physical and domestic well-being of children is evident across the political spectrum, from jingoism to socialism. On the far right can be found the imperialist schemes and reactionary polemics of Lord Brabazon, Earl of Meath. In the 1880s and 1890s, he lobbied for colonies for the unemployed, open spaces in cities, school playgrounds, the Children's Ministering League, state feeding of children and compulsory physical training. He was also involved with the Northern Union Schools of Cookery, the Housewifery Association, the National League for Physical Education and Improvement and the National Educational Union for harmonizing home and school training. At the same time, socialists on the school boards, like Margaret McMillan in Bradford and Annie Besant in London, were in the vanguard of campaigns for school welfare provision – free meals, detailed medical and dental examinations and reports by School Medical Officers, fumigation of verminous clothing, access to public baths, special provision for mentally deficient children, and so forth.[8]

Once again, the provision of welfare went hand in hand with the extension of surveillance and the gathering of information – the strategy of policing families. One of the most interesting formulations of the strategy, in that it also displays clearly a new conception of an organic state penetrating all areas of social life, can be found in the 'social imperialism' of the Fabian leaders Sidney and Beatrice Webb. For them, national efficiency required a number of interlocking changes: a rationalized administrative machinery, the improvement of industrial production by the application of scientific expertise (and hence the extension of scientific and technical education) and, again, the improvement of the nation's physique and the fitness of its population. In achieving them, education would be crucial. In 1901, Sidney Webb argued that in the new century, the primary duty of government would be considered 'the prevention of disease and premature death, and the building up of the nervous and muscular vitality of the race':

> As such, it must necessarily form the principal plank in any Imperial programme that will appeal to the Progressive instinct of the century. But it is not enough that we rear a physically healthy race. The policy of National Efficiency involves a great development of public education.[9]

For Webb this meant neither the board schools nor a return to 'the "common school" of our Radical grandfathers', but a rationalized and integrated system of public education, from primary schooling through selective secondary education to the universities. The key element here, in line with eugenist thinking of the time (from which he differed in other important ways), was selection. The man in the street, he wrote, 'will wake up if he is told that the whole system is to be so reorganized that every clever child, in every part of the country, shall get the best possible training that can be devised'.

Every *clever* child, not every child – for most children, he foresaw higher elementary schools which would not 'lead up to any higher *school*, but to the counting house, the factory, or the kitchen'.[10]

As chairman of the London Technical Education Board, Webb planned ' a number of specialized schools each more accurately fitting the needs of a particular section of children'; that is, secondary schooling based on scholarships. This is considered incompatible with the mechanical elementary education provided by the board schools. He also thought that the boards themselves were inefficient and too open to the influence of the teachers and Progressives, who found his commitment to selection uncongenial. He therefore made common cause with the Conservatives in Parliament, the Anglican wing of the Church and fellow enthusiasts for national efficiency, like the civil servant Robert Morant, in campaigning against the boards. The result was their abolition and the incorporation of education into the ambit of County Councils by the 1902 Balfour Education Act, which Morant steered through the Education Department. Webb's arguments for selective educational institutions were not based on political grounds alone, though. It was his assumptions about the psychological needs and capacities of individual children, and how these are distributed statistically through the population, that were pivotal. The outcome was a system based on segregation. Bright children, as identified by mental measurement, were to be separated from other children diagnosed as potentially dangerous or in danger, and therefore in need of care and control.

Does this brief account of the strategies for providing mass education proposed by people like Colquhoun, Kay-Shuttleworth and Webb help us to understand Sherlock Holmes's curious enthusiasm for the board schools? I think it does, at least to the extent they all reveal an emerging conception of popular education as a technique of government close to Foucault's notion of bio-politics or Jacques Donzelot's policing of families. The consistent aim is to moralize the working class – disciplining it, studying it, diagnosing its ills and inadequacies, tending to its welfare. In the course of the nineteenth century such interventions, initially religious or philanthropic, came more and more to be seen as the responsibility of the state. Or

FIGURE 1   The Lancastrian system in the early nineteenth century. Central School of the British and Foreign School Society, Borough Road, Southwark, London. (From the Society's *Manual of the System of Primary Instruction*, 1831.)

rather, it was in developing agencies to carry out such activities that the state emerges in its extended, governmental form. Holmes is merely, in effect, accepting the logic of Gramsci's axiom that 'the state must be conceived as an "educator", in as much as it tends precisely to create a new type or level of civilization'.[11] But this is to remain at the level of political metaphor. The way a problem is defined (here the management of the population) contains the supposed means of solving it (popular schooling). That tells us little about *how* it was supposed to work, let alone whether or not it succeeded. To understand that, it is necessary to turn from the strategic objectives articulated in educational ideologies to the subtle mechanisms of regulation and control operating in the daily routines of the schools.

Pedagogy

These mechanisms can be illustrated by re-running the history of nineteenth-century schooling from a different angle, highlighting

FIGURE 2 . Bell's Madras system. Central School of the National Society, Baldwin's Gardens, London, early nineteenth century. (From J. Hamel, *L'Enseignement Mutuel,* Paris 1818.)

now the techniques which rendered individual children the object of various forms of control, knowledge and concern.

There was nothing covert or mysterious about these techniques. They were built into the very structure and routine of the schools. Going back to the beginning of the century, consider the design of the monitorial schools and the forms of discipline and pedagogy it implied. Figure 1 shows a Lancastrian school. The master is on the right. The 'general monitor of order' stands on a stool in the centre, controlling some 365 boys all seated in long, fixed rows of desks. At the left-hand end of these are the 'monitors of class'. Figure 2 shows Bell's Madras system, in which the central area is kept clear. Classes are being given in three-sided, almost military formations, with pupils either standing or sitting on movable benches.[12]

Despite these differences, both are organized to allow instruction and control to pass through a series of relays — from master or mistress through the monitors to the pupils and back again. It is also clear that this form of surveillance depends on the visibility of the pupils to the master. The monitorial schools exemplify an architecture designed, in Foucault's words,

> to permit an internal, articulated and detailed control – to render visible those who are inside it; in more general terms, an architecture that would operate to transform individuals: to act on those it shelters, to provide a hold on their conduct, to carry the effects of power right to them, to make it possible to know them, to alter them.[13]

This link between Foucault's analysis and the monitorial schools can be made more concrete. In *Discipline and Punish*, Foucault attempts to show how, from the seventeenth and eighteenth centuries onwards, power has been directed at the production of regimented and self-policing subjects – 'docile bodies' is his phrase – through the pervasive, localized operation of a disciplinary technology. To illustrate the forms this technology had taken by the turn of the eighteenth and nineteenth centuries, Foucault refers to English reformers like Patrick Colquhoun and Jeremy Bentham.

From Bentham he takes his motif of the Panopticon, a design for a penitentiary in which a single observer in a watch-tower could watch over a circle of tiered, individual cells without being observed by the prisoners. The system was designed to produce an effect of constant, omniscient surveillance *within* the prisoners, even though not all of them would actually be watched all the time. It is no surprise, then, that Bentham enthusiastically supported the monitorial schools and was active in an ultimately fruitless scheme to found a school for the children of his Utilitarian friends using monitorial methods of discipline and a system of learning through rewards and punishments, and to be built according to 'the *Panopticon* principle of construction'.

In the Bell and Lancaster schools, the system of *hierarchical observation*, which Foucault identifies as one of the definitive techniques for implementing the new disciplinary power, was instituted in their design, the use of monitors and the systematic organization of pupils' time. Equally important, however, were new ways of studying, classifying and treating the inmates of the rationalized institutions. Just as the physical punishment of prisoners gave way to confinement and, increasingly, to programmes of rehabilitation based on information gathered about each case history – the technique of normative judgement – so the monitorial schools operated a detailed economy of punishments and rewards not only for pupils' ability to memorize their lessons, but also for their behaviour, attitude, time-keeping, cleanliness, and so on.

It was this devolved but coercive focus on the individual child that was criticized by educators like Kay-Shuttleworth and David Stow, a Christian philanthropist who wrote about teaching methods and ran a model school for training teachers in Glasgow. As Kay-Shuttleworth explained to the Select Committee on the Education of the Poorer Classes in 1838:

> I think that the opportunity for moral training among children during their usual associations in periods of recreation, and also while they are trained in the school, are greatly increased when they are in contact with numbers; and that although it may require a larger amount of intelligence and superior vigilance and activity on the part of the master, yet his opportunities, not merely of inculcating moral lessons, but forming good habits, are increased by the accidents which occur when numbers are assembled, and which develop the peculiarities of character, and especially the moral tendencies of different characters, rather than in a small school.

It was not enough to produce docile bodies through hierarchical observation. The civilizing goals of elementary education required pupils who could understand their lessons, and teachers who could act as ethical exemplars in whose 'moral observation' each child would find its own conscience. The solution was a move away from the individualism of the monitorial schools towards the simultaneous instruction of a whole class by the teacher.[11]

This new emphasis on what Stow called 'the sympathy of numbers' was reflected in changes to the design of school rooms. Whereas the desks in a Lancastrian school were often arranged in a slight incline to make all the pupils visible to the master, Stow introduced galleries designed to focus the attention of children on their teacher. Figure 3 shows an infant school room, designed by Stow, in this transitional phase. The boys and girls are seated on a gallery, with a wooden rail dividing them. In front of them stands

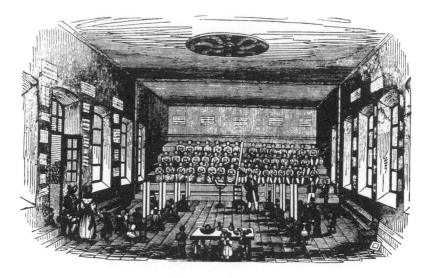

FIGURE 3   David Stow's model infants' school, 1836. (From Stow's
The Training System, 1836.)

the master, next to his chair and lectern. In the central part of the
room are lesson-posts with pictures or objects attached to them.
When not being taught in the gallery, the children would cluster
around these in groups to be taught by a monitor.[15]

What emerged under the name of simultaneous instruction was a
new combination of interrogatory methods with the grouping of
pupils using criteria which emphasized the similarities between
pupils in 'classes' rather than their individual differences. Through
these new methods, with pupils being asked questions randomly by
the teacher or being invited to indicate their readiness to answer by
putting up their hands, it was hoped that the minds of children
would be perpetually engaged and under the influence of the
master. No less important than what went on in the classroom, in
this view, was the playground – 'the principal scene of the real life of
children', according to Stow, and 'the arena on which their true
character and dispositions are exhibited'.[16]

By the time of the board schools in the 1870s the idea of the
school room had been replaced – or at least supplemented in larger

schools – by the characteristic design of a school consisting of a school hall surrounded by a number of separate classrooms. The London School Board was one of the first to appoint an architect, E.R. Robson, and in 1872 he laid down a number of principles and rules. Each group or 'standard' should be taught in a separate classroom, although 'as each school is under the supervision of one master or mistress, this principle must in some degree be subordinate to the necessity for such supervision'. All classrooms had to be entered from the central schoolroom. Boys and girls should be segregated as much as possible, using not only separate playgrounds but also separate entrances placed as far apart as possible – preferably on different streets. These principles are visible in the board school Robson designed in Wornington Road in the Portobello district of London in 1874, which also incorporated two infant school rooms and two babies' rooms in an elaborate ground-floor extension. The boys' and girls' schools were on the floors above; they show Robson moving towards the design based on a central hall with classrooms off it (see Figures 4 and 5).[17]

These designs and buildings are of more than architectural interest: they are monuments to changing pedagogic aspirations. For the reformers, however, it was not enough to change the schools. It was also vital to improve the status of teaching by turning it into a profession. The informal dame schools that offered little more than child-minding for urban working-class children were, according to the Newcastle Commission of 1861, 'a complete refuge for the destitute' run not only by poor widows but also by grocers, tobacconists, sailors, painters, housekeepers and ladies' maids. It was to overcome this problem that the monitorial 'engine of instruction' was designed as far as possible to be teacher-proof, and it was against this utilitarian reduction of the teacher to overseer that Stow and Kay-Shuttleworth were reacting. That system might have allowed 'sound instruction', complained Stow, but not 'physical, intellectual, and moral training': 'Schools are not so constructed as to enable the child to be superintended in real life at play; the master has not the opportunity of training, except under the *unnatural* restraint of a covered schoolroom.' The playground and simultaneous instruction provided opportunities for the master to

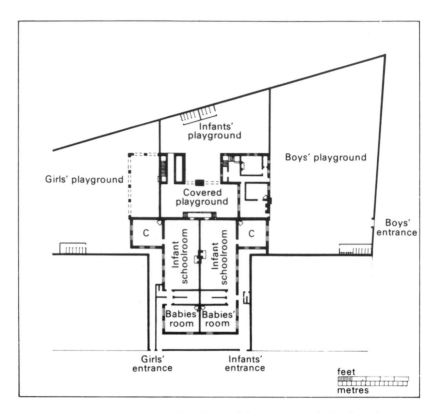

FIGURE 4   Wornington Road Board School, Portobello, London.
The infants' department on the ground floor, 1874. (From M. Seaborne
and R. Lowe, *The English School: Its Architecture and Organization, Vol. 2
1870–1970*, London 1977.)

provide moral guidance, and this in turn required a quite new form
of understanding and sympathy in which the child's confidence
sustains the teacher's authority, thereby reinforcing his status as
moral exemplar:

> Whilst the pupils sympathise with each other, it is important that the
> children sympathise with their master. For this purpose, it is necessary
> that he place himself on such terms with his pupils as that they can,
> without fear, make him their confidant, unburden their minds, and tell
> him any little story, or mischievous occurrence.

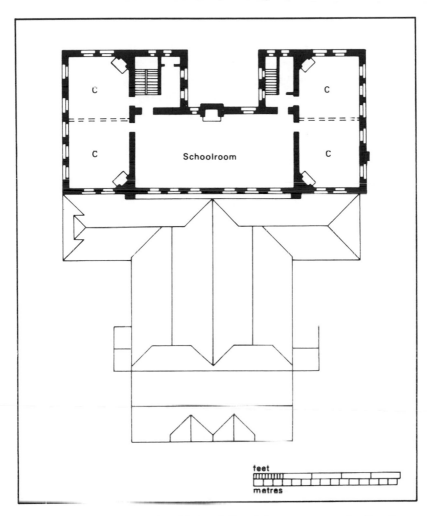

FIGURE 5 Wornington Road School. Boys' department on the first floor.

How were this new social status and this special type of personality to be formed? For Kay-Shuttleworth, this was the decisive question. The former required that training be taken out of the hands of the religious denominations and into those of the government, so that teachers could become better qualified, better paid (with a proper pension), and so raised in public esteem. Pupils aged between thirteen and eighteen were to be apprenticed to masters; then they could compete for scholarships to two-year courses in the new residential training colleges like the one he established at Battersea. Here he tried to recreate the monastic, Rousseauian ruralism of De Fellenberg and Vehril's institution at Hofwyl in Switzerland, by which he had been greatly impressed. Trainees milked and looked after cows, tended pigs, cultivated the gardens and subsisted on a plain diet.

As in the schools, the colleges concentrated on the formation of a moral and humble self-regulation through minute surveillance under the benevolent guidance of the Principal:

> The Principal should be *wise as a serpent*, while the gentleness of his discipline, and his affectionate solicitude for the well-being of his pupils, should encourage the most unreserved communications with him.... As far as its relation to the Principal only is concerned, every fault should be restrained and corrected by a conviction of the pain and anxiety which it causes to an anxious friend, rather than by the fear of a too jealous authority. Thus conscience will gradually be roused by the example of a master, respected for his purity, and loved for his gentleness, and inferior sentiments will be replaced by motives derived from the highest source.

The training of the teacher's intellect took second place to this moral regime. Indeed, too great an intellectual development might lead to a vanity and dissatisfaction incompatible with the teacher's 'humble and subordinate position'. Although 'master of his school', to his superiors he should remain 'an intelligent servant and minister'.[18]

This demand for an exemplary humility seems to have been one factor that led, especially in the 1860s, to trained teachers leaving the job for less demanding and better paid alternatives; many became office workers or railway clerks. At the same time, the Newcastle Commission found that the voluntary schools had failed to serve as moral lighthouses in the urban ghettos. Most of the teachers were untrained and uncertified; many were pupil-teachers. It was not freedom, reciprocal sympathy and moral observation that usually characterized teacher–pupil relations, but a far from subtle regime of corporal punishment and intimidation. This is in part what lay behind the switch from the critical guidance and support of HMI to the accountancy of the Revised Code.

That teachers turned out to be mechanical disciplinarians rather than moral exemplars was just one symptom of the failure of moral environmentalism. This raised the question whether simultaneous instruction was the most appropriate method for popular education. Towards the end of the century, a new approach was embodied in the physical separation of classrooms in the board schools then being built, and the phrase 'classroom teachers' began to be used for the first time. These adult teachers, often qualified women drawn in by the demand created by the 1870 Education Act, were now under the control of a head teacher. A new pedagogy was also emerging in university departments of education and in professional journals. In his *Principles of Class Teaching* (1902), for example, J.J. Findlay (who was to become Professor of Education at Manchester University) expressed his belief that the '*unit in Education* is not the school, or the class, but *the single pupil*'.[19]

Feeding into this professional, child-centred discipline of pedagogy were two other discourses concerned with the scientific classification of children: child study and mental measurement. The vogue for child study represented an attempt to chart systematic patterns of growth in children. Drawing on a mixture of biology and everyday common sense, the published studies often took the form of detailed accounts by scientists of their observations of their own children's 'development' – their physical growth, their beliefs and habits, their play, and so on. Studies like Wilhelm Preyer's *The Mind of a Child*, which appeared in English in 1881, or Charles Darwin's *A Biographical Sketch of an Infant* (1887) did not only impute a normal process of growth to children. They are important above all because they singled out for the first time children *as a category* for scientific study. Mental measurement was not concerned with the overall development of children. Its sole concern was with their intellectual capacities or 'intelligence' and its distribution across a population. For Francis Galton, the leading exponent of this new science, the impetus for such work was the eugenist fear about degeneracy and a desire to protect and improve the quality of the English population.

John Pedley

FIGURES 6 AND 7   The Stockport Ragged and Industrial School.
Cartes-de-visite, *c.*1865.

Martha Berry

Once again, we are confronted with that sea-change in the modes of understanding and political action in the decades around the turn of the century, in which the capacities of individual children, as defined by the new psychological sciences, feed into a new pedagogy and ever more pervasive forms of social welfare, investigation and surveillance.[20]

The various pedagogies and disciplines I have described indicate how a population is regulated. Its anonymous mass has first to be broken down into individual cases, so that these can then be regrouped around statistical norms: hence the monitoring of children, their moral observation, or the scientific study of their development. Each student – like every prisoner and every patient – was ascribed a history in the material form of often minutely detailed institutional records and reports. This suggests a new perspective on the role of examinations in education. The norms or standards defined in the Revised Code of 1862, for example, were in part a somewhat crude mechanism to control what went on in the schools – critics have, of course, noted the similarities in today's National Curriculum. But the routine testing of pupils' performance also established a hierarchical order among them and allowed an identity to be constructed around their development, their aptitudes, and their qualifications.

The records kept on pupils – particularly those considered to be in danger morally or potentially dangerous socially – were doubtless modelled on the files kept by the police and by prisons. In both cases, new technologies like photography became part of the proliferating archive. Its images were invested with the power to show the true nature not only of criminality, but also of insanity, poverty, poor housing, and so forth. In the 1860s, the Stockport Ragged and Industrial School commissioned a local photographer to compile an album of each of the teachers and children in the school, and in 1874, Dr Barnardo opened a Photographic Department in his Home for Destitute Lads in Stepney. The role of the pictures was clear:

> to obtain and retain an exact likeness of each child and enable them, when it is attached to his history, to trace the child's career.... By

Admitted January 5th, 1876.

Aged 16 *Years.*

Height, 4-*ft.* 11-*in.*

Color of { *Hair, Dark Brown.*
{ *Eyes, Brown.*

Complexion, Dark.

Marks on body—None.

If Vaccinated—Right Arm.

If ever been in a Reformatory or Industrial School ? No.

FIGURE 8   Section of a *Personal History* of a child at Dr Barnardo's
Homes, 1874–83.

means of these likenesses children absconding from our Homes are often recovered and brought back, and in not a few instances juveniles who have been stolen from their parents and guardians or were tempted by evil companions to leave home, and at last, after wondering for a while on the streets, found their way to our Institution, have been recognized by parents or friends and finally restored to their care.

With the coming of compulsory education, the school became a relay in extending both surveillance and welfare provision into the community. The progressive London School Board, for example, appointed a network of Visitors to counteract truancy and to 'police' the families of working-class children more generally by providing information (not only about educational matters) which could be tapped by local and national government authorities. As early as 1875, the Visitors were asked to prepare a census of the wife desertion they discovered in the course of their duties.[21]

Architecture, pedagogy, scientific studies of 'the child', examinations, written and photographic records, pastoral intervention: these are some of the 'subtle mechanisms' through which education was designed to individuate people, discipline them, and render them the objects of tutelage and pastoral supervision. I stress *designed*, because it should not be assumed that these mechanisms actually worked. Accused by an interviewer of producing too neat and conflict-free an account of bio-power, Foucault himself cheerfully admitted the danger:

> Oh, I quite agree. Judiciary and psychiatry join hands, but only after such a mess, such a shambles! Only my position is as if I were dealing with a battle: if one isn't content with descriptions, if one wants to try and explain a victory or a defeat, then one does have to pose the problems in terms of strategies, and ask, 'Why did that work? How did that hold up?' That's why I look at things from this angle, which may end up giving the impression the story is too pretty to be true.[22]

What a Foucauldian approach can reveal with great clarity is what is sometimes referred to as 'the hidden curriculum': the principles governing the organization of schooling and its forms of discipline and pedagogy. This always strikes me as an odd phrase, because the shape of the schoolroom, the style of the teacher and the forms of behaviour demanded of pupils, far from being hidden, make up the normal experience of schooling. Perhaps it is this obviousness that makes it possible to overlook them. Rather more mysterious – and equally important for understanding the shambles of educational history – is what goes on in the formal curriculum: how it embodies a particular ordering of the symbolic, and how this then plays into the ordering of subjectivity.

Curriculum

I noted earlier the Tory politician Robert Lowe's scepticism about the social and political benefits of popular education, at least when presented as part of the strategy of moral environmentalism. For him, the limited steps towards democracy through the extension of male suffrage in the 1860s brought about a dramatic change of heart. They made it necessary, in his famous phrase, to 'compel our future masters to learn their letters'. He now advocated universal, compulsory education.

Lowe spelt out the logic behind his new position in *Primary and Classical Education* (1867). Whereas Kay-Shuttleworth and Stow wanted to embody cultural authority in the pastoral figure of the teacher, Lowe saw the hierarchies of symbolic value embodied in a differentiated curriculum as the normative cultural referent in relation to which children would play out the transferential drama of their school career. He therefore argued that, if the lower classes were to have *political* power, then the higher must develop the potential of this *cultural* power. They should use their 'greater intelligence and leisure' to ensure that they 'know the things the working men know, only know them infinitely better in their principles and in their details'. By instituting this new pattern of cultural authority in this way, they might 'conquer back by means of a wider and more enlightened cultivation some of the influence which they have lost by political change'. Lowe's strategy was thus to institute clear ideological boundaries between the bourgeoisie and the newly enfranchised lower classes. That is why the latter should 'be educated that they appreciate and defer to a higher cultivation when they meet it; and the higher classes ought to be educated in a very different manner, in order that they may exhibit to the lower classes that higher education to which, if it were shown to them, they would bow down and defer.'[23]

In some comments on education in 1970, Foucault offers what could be a gloss on this strategy: 'Any system of education is a political way of maintaining or modifying the appropriation of discourses, along with the knowledges and powers which they carry,' he observes. And this 'social appropriation of discourses' always takes place along lines 'marked out by social distances, oppositions and struggles'. Thus Lowe did not propose a separate curriculum for children from different classes. He wanted to institute a different *manner* of education and a different *orientation* towards knowledge. It was less the manifest content of syllabuses that mattered than the cultural rules embodied in what was taught and how it was taught: those implicit rules that define what is true, what is relevant, what is normal, what is valuable and who has the right to give voice to a particular discourse. If popular schooling did produce the sort of deference that Lowe desired (and that is, of course, open to question), it would not be because pupils necessarily believed what their books told them about the inevitability of their humble lot and the superiority of their race. Rather, the classification and framing of knowledge in the curriculum set in place a hierarchy of symbolic forms which are enacted and negotiated in differentiated modes of agency. The instrumental and mechanical forms of language and literature in the elementary schools are more disciplinary, for example, than the authoritative appropriation of literary language and idealist patterns of taste in the grammar and public schools.[24]

This is how the curriculum differentiates and categorizes people. It specifies what it is to be educated, cultivated, discriminating, clever, and so forth, and, when linked to psychological notions of development and cognition, it enables such characteristics to appear as the natural aptitudes of the people so defined. This is why I shall be returning more than once to the question of literacy, for the relationship between the speaking subject and the forms of language and writing transmitted by the school provides a key instance of the dynamics between the pedagogic and the performative.

*

In the next chapter, I pursue these themes around the institution and negotiation of cultural authority in relation to the categories of *literature* and *the popular*. Here, I have tried to show why the institution schooling cannot be adequately explained either by the psychological narrative of development or by the sociological narrative of socialization. The pedagogic techniques and disciplinary practices developed in the nineteenth century are better understood as technologies of government. Operating on the cusp of the public and the private, their aim was to turn children into good citizens whose competences, tastes and consciences would be attuned to broader socio-political objectives. I have not examined the often unformulated and unrecognized ways in which pupils confront and negotiate this pervasive ethical machinery. That does not mean that I assume that the deployment of the norms within apparatuses like education is sufficient to ensure that they *do* appear at the heart of our interior being, or that the visibility of the subject to panoptic power guarantees that the identity ascribed is the identity experienced. On the contrary, pupils' tactics of reinterpretation, resistance, rejection and overinvestment suggest both how the deployment of social and symbolic norms structures their field of action, but also that they are not simply internalized. It is this disjuncture between the pedagogic and the performative that reveals the paradox of the Foucauldian account:

> the model of self-surveillance implicitly recalls the psychoanalytic model of moral conscience even as the resemblance is being disavowed. The image of self-surveillance, self-correction, is both required to construct the subject and made redundant by the fact that the subject thus constructed is, by definition, absolutely upright, completely correct.[25]

The danger, in other words, is that subjectivity may be misread as an identity, or even multiple identities, which reflect an external order. The real mystery that has yet to be solved lies in the dynamics of translation, displacement, repression and transgression characterizing an apparently paradoxical process: the structuring of agency.

2

HOW ENGLISH IS IT?

Popular Literature and National Culture

Some feel we are in danger of losing our British heritage and national pride and we do not intend to go down this path in Berkshire.

> Tory councillors, on scrapping Berkshire's policy
> on racial equality in education, 1988

If the body of objects we study – the corpus formed by works of literature – belongs to, gains coherence from, and in a sense emanates out of the concept of nation, nationality, and even of race, there is very little in contemporary critical discourse making these actualities possible as subjects of discussion.

> Edward Said

At the end of the previous chapter, I raised briefly two issues that are important for my argument about education as an apparatus of government. I suggested that the school curriculum sets in place a particular disposition of cultural authority. I also stressed that this authority only becomes a reality as it is negotiated and reworked by its consumers, the pupils. Here, I explore that cultural dynamic between the pedagogic and the performative in more detail, although approaching it from a different, somewhat oblique angle.

Given the nexus of literature, nation and race identified by Edward Said, my question is what role *popular* literature plays in the formation of a *national* culture. Although education is not at the forefront of the argument, my premiss is that in practice the linkage between the categories of literature, nation and race is achieved largely through their dissemination by the institutions of education. The canon of national Literature is defined, reproduced and modified as it is taught to succeeding generations in schools and universities. That is how its status within the national culture is established. Equally, though, in a mutually reinforcing movement, this academic authority is ascribed to English Literature's expressive relationship to the nation and the people. Ever since the curriculum was consolidated in its modern form, Literature has been supposed to articulate the nation's shared imaginative past, those values and narratives that make up 'our' common cultural heritage. It has proved to be one of the most enduring of those traditions of Englishness invented in the decades around the turn of the century in response to the extension of democracy that Robert Lowe nervously identified and to the domestic consequences of England's imperial power.[1]

Rather than pursuing the argument through the history of the curriculum, I approach the cultural ambivalence of popular literature from two directions. In the first part of the chapter, I show how the social institution of Literature comes to organize the field of writing, and why the category of popular literature is both a necessity and a problem for it. It is necessary because it marks a boundary between what is and what is not Literature; the popular is in this sense the constitutive outside of Literature. At the same time, it is a problem because these excluded forms of writing reveal the splits and fragmentations in the nation-people whose unity is supposedly expressed by Literature.

In the second part of the chapter, I try to suggest how all this looks from the other side, from the side of the popular and of reading. Although, as readers, we act within a semantic field structured by the evaluative categories established by Literature, we *do* act. Popular reading, Michel de Certeau insists in *The Practice of Everyday Life*, is never passive. It involves invention, improvisation and resourcefulness. Whether it be a novel, newspaper or television programme, 'to read is to wander through an imposed system (that of the text, analogous to the constructed order of a city or of a supermarket)'. In our reading we make that imposed structure habitable, rather as we furnish a rented apartment with our own acts and memories and designs. At the same time as making an argument about the sort of fantasy scenarios that are built into popular fictions, therefore, I also try to enact the sort of *bricolage* or recombination that de Certeau ascribes to popular reading. My aim is to bring out the transgressive and recursive practices of everyday life through which people negotiate the authoritative cultural narratives of the book, the cinema or the school.[2]

National Culture and Popular Literature

Culture, says Edward Said, refers to what is at stake in the phrases *belonging to* or *in a* place, being *at home in a place*. This emphasis on place may be a poignant index of Said's own displacement in the Palestinian diaspora, but it does underline the almost tautological nature of the concept 'national culture'. 'The nation' is itself, in Benedict Anderson's phrase, an 'imagined community' – in other words, the symbolic universe in which we feel at home. As the Palestinian example shows, the bonds of national solidarity are not wholly dependent on the territorial existence of a nation-state. What is essential is the representation of mutually anonymous and potentially hostile populations as 'the people', heirs to a common past and subjects of a shared destiny. This expansive version of nationalism, Anderson argues, became possible in post-medieval Europe as the result of the spread of vernacular languages, literacy and forms of communication based on print technology, notably the novel and the newspaper.[3]

For Anderson, therefore, nationalism is better compared to kinship and religion than to liberalism or fascism. It is a mentality rather than an ideology. I would suggest a slightly different, three-way distinction between, first, specific nationalist ideologies (whether imperialist, isolationist or liberationist); second, a communality figured as a narrative of nationhood (Anderson's imagined community); and, third, the apparatus of discourses and technologies (print capitalism, education, mass media and so forth) which *produces* what is generally recognized as 'the national culture'. This third aspect implies that 'the nation' is an effect of these cultural technologies, not their origin. A nation does not express itself through its culture. It is culture that produces 'the nation', but always as if it were anterior to these processes of production. What is produced is neither an identity nor a single consciousness, but hierarchically organized values, dispositions and differences. This heterogeneity is given a certain fixity as 'the nation' differentiates it from other cultures by marking its boundaries. This integrity can only constitute a fictional unity, of course, because the 'us' on the inside is itself always differentiated.

Take as a small example of this internal differentiation and drawing of external boundaries the concluding remarks from a radio talk – on the Third Programme, of course – which Lord Keynes gave in 1945. He was speaking in his role as chairman of the newly established Arts Council of Great Britain, a state institution designed to police cultural values within a national framework and protect them from the decline of private patronage and the hostility of the marketplace:

> How satisfactory it would be if different parts of the country would again walk their several ways as they once did and learn to develop something different from their neighbours and characteristic of themselves. Nothing can be more damaging than the excessive prestige of metropolitan standards and fashions. Let every part of Merry England be merry in its own way. Death to Hollywood![4]

Keynes is proposing something not dissimilar to Gramsci's concept of a national-popular culture. It looks rather different, however, when seen from the chair at the head of the Arts Council table rather than from the fascist prison cell in which Gramsci fashioned his vision of it. Keynes acknowledges differences within the nation but, disavowing his own mandarin metropolitanism, domesticates them as diversity rather than antagonism. He draws them into a unity by contrasting his version of the organically popular (Merry England) to a different image of the popular as a threat to its boundaries – the alien mass culture of the old bogey Hollywood.

In a case like Keynes's Merry England/Hollywood binarism, the relationship between *national* and *popular* represents a high/low or positive/negative opposition. But, at the same time, he presents the two terms as synonymous – the national culture speaking to and for the English people. Underlying both usages is a tension between the fixity of the national and the plurality or heterogeneity of the popular. In Bakhtin's terms, culture can be seen as a force-field in

51

which identity, standard speech and the state exert a centripetal pull against the centrifugal forces of cultural difference, linguistic variation and carnival. The popular does not simply represent either the centripetal or the centrifugal pole. It reproduces the tension between them. Centripetal agencies (whether Keynes and the Arts Council or Gramsci and the Communist Party) attempt to impose their competing conceptions of a unified people-nation onto a fragmentary and differentiated population.

How does literature – and particularly popular literature – fit into this model? Said claims that literature 'belongs to, gains coherence from, and in a sense emanates out of the concept of nation, nationality, and even of race'. By this, he probably means in part that literary writing formulates the characteristic chronotopes of a national mentality. He may also be making the historical point that the literary forms of the European languages provided the medium for the definition and diffusion of national vernaculars, in opposition to the transnational jargon of Latin and sub-national regional dialects. In this process, the imposition of a correct or standard national language established new patterns of linguistic differenti- ation and brought into being the new institution of Literature. In the British context, for example, the emergence of English as an academic discipline and a school subject, and the fixing of the national language (which was in effect literary language) in the *Oxford English Dictionary* ensured that, by the latter part of the nineteenth century, Literature had been instituted as the point of reference around which relationships of difference and similarity within the field of writing were organized.[5] It became a centripetal force within the field of the national culture, especially as the post- Disraelian organic state was extending new forms of govern- mentality throughout civil society.

The institutionalization of Literature in Britain in the nineteenth century can also be seen as one response to changing political perceptions of the potential dangers of popular literacy; these were closely bound up with the changing educational strategies I outlined in the previous chapter. In the period between Paine's *Rights of Man* and the rise of Chartism, these dangers had been seen in terms of political radicalism. In the course of the century, however, literacy lost its threatening aspect and became, as Robert Lowe perceived, a means of 'educating our future masters'. Increasingly, it was *illiteracy* and a taste for debased, sensational fiction that were identified as pathological symptoms. The illiterate became the target of the 'administered' forms in which the standard language and the national literature were taught in the elementary schools set up after Forster's Education Act in 1870. This shift, within the politics of literacy, from a rhetoric of power and confrontation to discourses of cultural pathology was evident in changing strategies around publishing for the people. In 1819, for example, the Utilitarian publisher Charles Knight noted the influence of the radical press. 'There is a *new power in society,*' he wrote, and warned that contemporary journals like Cobbett's *Political Register* and Wooler's *Black Dwarf* had 'combined to give that power a direction. The work must be taken out of their hands.' When the *Boy's Own Paper* was first published sixty years later by the Religious Tract Society, its aim was to provide '*healthy boy literature* to counteract the vastly increasing circulation of illustrated and other papers of a bad tendency'.[6]

It was through such strategies of nation building and governmentality that language and literature took on political importance. Even today they retain this potency for the One-Nation strand of English Conservatism: they are intimately bound up with its central idea of cultural authority as social cement. In November 1986, for example, Kenneth Baker, as Secretary of State for Education, was preparing to introduce a National Curriculum into English and Welsh schools. In a lecture he developed his ideas about language, literature and national identity:

> Next to our people, the English language is our greatest asset as a nation, it is the essential ingredient of the Englishness of England.... [I]t is the people of England who fashion the shape, create the flavour and determine the direction of our changing national consciousness. The thing that has held them together over the centuries and would still allow an Englishman transported back a hundred years or two hundred years or four hundred years, if you have a good ear for accent, to recognize that he was in the same country, is the English language.

Here is Englishness as heritage, as mythical identity, as the sensual experience of an imagined past embodied not just in the language, but in the English countryside, in certain styles of architecture, and in English Literature. In this vision, Literature not only produces for the individual 'that sense of engagement with a common humanity' (or at least those parts of it that speak English), it is also necessary for the health of the nation. 'A society whose imagination is retarded or stagnating is a society which is looking at a bleak future.' Mr Baker's invocation of England as an organic community recalls the terms in which a century earlier, in the 1860s, Richard Chevenix Trench, Dean of Westminster and prime instigator of what became the *Oxford English Dictionary*, had justified his project:

> If the great acts of that nation to which we belong are precious to us, if we feel ourselves made greater by their greatness, summoned to a nobler life by the nobleness of Englishmen who have already lived and died ... what can more clearly point out their native land and ours as having fulfilled a glorious past, as being destined for a glorious future, than that they should have acquired for themselves and for those who came after them a clear, a strong, an harmonious, a noble language?

In the 1980s, Kenneth Baker likewise concluded that 'our children' should learn from studying English 'the confidence that comes from knowing that the language belongs to them and is in their keeping for the time being, and that is both a reassuring and awesome prospect.' Language, then, is simultaneously external and internal to the speaking subject. It is both pedagogic, in teaching them the awesome responsibility of being English, and performative, in that it is only through their speech that the nation is given voice and so redeemed.

From the inception of mass education, the external, pedagogic dimension of language has been given its most authoritative expression in Literature. Retrospectively, it provides the criteria for selecting certain texts as the canon. Programmatically, it calls for a vernacular national literature – usually, as Benedict Anderson observes, in the form of the realist novel.

Where then does popular literature fit into this model? The term implies a residue left over after true Literature has been defined. Often, it refers to the formulaic genres that people actually choose to read: 'railway fiction' to while away a journey, holiday reading for the beach, pornography for titillation or Jeffrey Archer as a soporific. Occasionally, it means specifically working-class forms of writing or modes of reading.[7] But the axiom that popular literature is failed Literature still dominates, and limits, analysis. Pessimistic cultural critics treat it as a conduit for 'dominant ideologies'. Ignoring a book's formal or narrational properties, they will gut it for its ideological content. 'How sexist is it?' they ask. 'How racist is it? How imperialist?' The optimists, meanwhile, see popular literature as a carnival of literary subversion, a centrifugal force ripe for political exploitation.

The trouble with both these (not terribly caricatured) approaches is that their Literature/popular fiction distinction remains within the terms of aesthetic and ethical evaluation set up by the category of Literature – authenticity, autonomy, and so forth. What I am proposing instead is a historical understanding of the discursive and institutional relationships between 'national', 'popular' and 'Literature'. From this point of view, popular literature appears neither as ideological commodity nor as populist subversion. Instead, it can be understood as a normative category, which renders the diversity of fictional texts and modes of reading manageable. It allows these to be incorporated within the hierarchy of values and differentiations that constitute both the institution Literature and the national culture.

This triangulating conception of national/popular/Literature calls into question not only the idea of Literature as the expression of the nation, but also the old oppositions of Literature/popular fiction and high culture/mass culture. That is not to say these categorical oppositions have no cultural effects. On the contrary, Fredric Jameson is quite right to insist that they are 'objectively related and dialectically interdependent phenomena'. For him, though, the high pole in literary culture is represented neither by a national canon (the Englishness of Quiller-Couch or its American equivalent) nor by realism, but by those forms of writing which resist the commodification of literature. That, he says, means *modernism*. Laura Kipnis takes this further, suggesting that the high culture/mass culture binarism is a precondition for the existence of modernism: 'Dismantling the ideological scaffold of modernism allows the rereading of modernism as constituted solely within this split, and existing only so long as it could keep its Other – the popular, the low, the regional and the impure – at bay.'[8]

It is true that towards the end of the nineteenth century, at about the time Literature was being institutionalized in the education system and popular literature was being pathologized, the appearance of aestheticism, decadence and symbolism signalled the arrival of a recognizably modernist literary aesthetic. It is also true, however, that the modernism/mass culture polarity has always been far less stable than Jameson and Kipnis imply: think only of Eisenstein's enthusiasm for Hollywood and Mickey Mouse, the surrealists' championing of the tackiest forms of popular culture, the European intelligentsia's enduring love affair with jazz, or the recycling of popular imagery in Pop Art. Many forms of modernism were, at least to begin with, profoundly hostile towards existing aesthetic and political institutions. The history of modernism, certainly in the visual arts, has been a cyclical one in which anti-institutional moments of formation are followed by a consolidation into schools and traditions, which leads in turn to breaks from the by now institutionalized forms. In literature, modernism has been identified as a source of opposition to the literary parochialism of English academic culture around the turn of the century, which provoked a mutation in critical ideology. But then, of course, it was also the medium of Pound and Eliot. The simple point is that modernism can be, and has been, either 'pro' or 'anti' *both* high culture and popular culture. Equally, the history of modernism makes it quite obvious that it cannot have only one fixed political meaning. It has been championed and anathematized with equal vigour both on the Right and on the Left (where it has been seen as everything from the 'revolution of the word' to a CIA plot).[9]

The importance of modernism here is that it represents an alternative point of cultural authority to that of the academy. It was instituted and sustained more through a network of literary and art markets, journalism and funding agencies, whether those of private patrons or government bodies. It has always had a deeply ambivalent relationship to academic culture, to national cultures and to popular cultures. The case of modernism thus underlines the inherent indeterminacy and contestability of even authoritative centripetal categories within the force-field of culture. By the same token, in purely conceptual terms, there is nothing necessarily progressive about the popular, nor inherently reactionary about the national. But then, of course, categories like Literature, nation and people are never *purely* conceptual. They exist historically only as they are articulated in education, publishing, the mass media and the other components of the pedagogic apparatus. That is why I am arguing for a move away from that style of ideological critique that simply measures the progressiveness or reactionariness of a given text, genre or movement. Rather than stay within the terms of reference of the apparatus, it is more important to analyse the regulation of the semantic field as one aspect of the policing of a population.[10]

This approach pays special attention to the definition and maintenance of publics, interpretive communities, the people-nation. That is why literacy and Literature are at the heart of the academic curriculum. They constitute the symbolic mode through which the pedagogies and disciplines of schooling that I described in the previous chapter are enacted. This, then, is how the authoritative currency of Literature emanates from and in the same movement enunciates the categories of nationality and race. But that is only half an answer to Said's conundrum. It begs another question: what is people's subjective investment in the representations produced by these cultural technologies? Do the pleasures of reading popular fiction also emanate from and sustain nationality and race? And if so, how?

Popular Reading: Fantasy and *Bricolage*

In exploring the readerly aspects of the links between literature, nation and race, my aim is not to define a new canon as a populist alternative to the official canon. Nor am I proposing a rationalist pedagogy that would save readers from the ideological stupefaction of trash fiction. The old images of popular culture as either repressed voices in need of liberation or false consciousness being inscribed onto dopey readers are both equally condescending and equally inaccurate. Mine is a different question: how certain categories, values and narratives are disseminated through the activity of reading, and especially how these reappear in the folded or crumpled form of fantasy, desire and anxiety.

Such processes are investigated with some ingenuity by Peter Stallybrass and Allon White in *The Politics and Poetics of Transgression.* Particularly relevant to my argument is their account of the way that cultural low-Others become an eroticized constituent of fantasy life. In the 'inner dynamic of the boundary constructions necessary to collective identity', they suggest, these Others cannot simply be excluded. They remain a troublesome presence for an official culture, returning in the form of the *grotesque*; or rather in its two forms. The first is 'the grotesque as the "Other" of the defining group or self'. Distinct from this is 'the grotesque as a boundary phenomenon of hybridization or inmixing, in which self and other become enmeshed in an inclusive, heterogeneous, dangerously unstable zone':

> a fundamental mechanism of identity formation *produces* the second, hybrid grotesque at the level of the political unconscious *by the very struggle to exclude the first grotesque....* The point is that the *exclusion* necessary to the formation of social identity at [one] level is simultaneously a *production* at the level of the Imaginary, and a production, what is more, of a complex hybrid fantasy emerging out of the very attempt to demarcate boundaries, to unite and purify the social collectivity.[11]

This can only ever be an *attempted* demarcation. The boundaries remain permeable; the 'inside' is always fragmented and differentiated rather than pure and united. This helps to explain the ambivalent 'repugnance and fascination' evident in representations of the low-Other. To illustrate the point, Stallybrass and White quote Edward Said's argument that the political discourse of Orientalism 'depends for its strategy on [a] flexible *positional* superiority, which puts the Westerner in a whole series of possible relationships with the Orient without ever losing the upper hand.' What is at stake in this play of 'identity' and 'otherness' is establishing boundaries as a condition of knowledge and of identity: 'European culture gained in strength and identity by setting itself off against the Orient as a sort of . . . underground self.'[12]

Reading this sparked off in me a train of thought about how boundaries of both racial and sexual difference are staged not only by certain recurring scenarios in popular fiction, but also in the *practices* of popular reading. In its silent and heterodox reworking of texts, Michel de Certeau argues, reading is ironic and transgressive. 'Readers are like travellers; they move across lands belonging to someone else, like nomads poaching their way across fields they did not write.' As an example of this displacement and impertinence, he cites the way that Barthes reads Proust in Stendhal's text. Similarly, the place of a reader in relation to a popular text is not '*here* or *there*, one or the other, but neither the one nor the other, simultaneously inside and outside, dissolving both by mixing them together.'[13] It is in this spirit of foraging and recombination that I see emerging through Said's account of the relationship between West and Orient a ghostly but gaudy image. Sax Rohmer's *The Mystery of Dr. Fu Manchu* is one of the most irredeemably and dementedly racist works in English popular literature. But doesn't the colonial policeman Nayland Smith's description of Fu Manchu provide an uncannily apt example of the simultaneous revulsion and fascination provoked by the grotesque?

> 'Imagine a person, tall, lean and feline, high-shouldered, with a brow like Shakespeare, a close-shaven skull, and long, magnetic eyes of the true cat-green. Invest him with all the cruel cunning of an entire Eastern race, accumulated in one giant intellect, with all the resources of science past and present, with all the resources, if you will, of a wealthy government – which, however, already has denied all knowledge of his existence. Imagine that awful being, and you have a mental picture of Dr. Fu Manchu, the yellow peril incarnate in one man.'[14]

What fascination might this characterization have held for the petty-bourgeois commuter in his railway carriage in 1913 who seems to be its implicit addressee? The key is surely Said's symbolic opposition of West to East across which the book's characters and relationships are plotted. Rather than representing a self-contained identity (Englishness), which is then contrasted with other, equally coherent, identities (here Chineseness), *Fu Manchu* enunciates the split in identity that is the ground of racial difference. 'The head of the Yellow movement' provides a necessary horizon to the identity of 'the man who fought on behalf of the entire white race' (p. 104). No Fu Manchu, no Nayland Smith: the potentially infinite and so terrifying plenitude of absolute difference is thus domesticated as a comic-strip polarity.

The appeal of popular genres is that they are both stereotyped and infinitely variable. They incorporate contingent topical material into a fixed repertoire of narrative structures. So *Fu Manchu* repeats the familiar trope of the 'evil genius' masterminding the metropolitan underworld. Like Professor Moriarty or Fantômas, Fu Manchu seems to figure the social tensions and anxieties of city life – but in archaic form. The modern fear of the irruption of the irrational within everyday normality (the monsters produced by Goya's 'sleep of reason', Baudelaire's 'savagery that lurks in the midst of civilization') is thus linked to a historically specific paranoia about the 'return' of the alien. Within the discursive field of post-imperialism, which seems to appear in popular fiction at the time of the Boer War, this invasive alien is *produced* as grotesque through its attempted *exclusion*:[15]

> Ideal rural peace, and the music of an English summer evening; but to my eyes, every shadow holding fantastic terrors; to my ears, every sound a signal of dread. For the deathful hand of Fu-Manchu was stretched over Redmoat, at any hour to loose strange, Oriental horrors upon its inmates. (p. 53)

This logic of exclusion and return recalls both the ambivalence between censorship and figuration that underlies the excesses of fantastic fictions and also Julia Kristeva's idea of the abject: 'What disturbs identity, system, order. What does not respect borders, positions, rules.' In *Fu Manchu*, eugenicist fears about the purity of the social collectivity (the white race) and perennial anxieties about the irruption of the abject are condensed into in a viral imagery – 'a menace to Europe and to America greater than the plague' (p. 108) – and also into an imagery of pervasive mists and aromas:[16]

A breeze whispered through the leaves; a great wave of exotic perfume
swept from the open window towards the curtained doorway. It was a
breath of the East – that stretched out a yellow hand to the West. It was
symbolic of the subtle, intangible power manifested in Dr. Fu-Manchu,
as Nayland Smith – lean, agile, bronzed with the suns of Burma – was
symbolic of the clean British efficiency which sought to combat the
insidious enemy. (p. 86)

What determines the form of the adaptable but consistent
narratives of popular genres? Freud suggested that at the heart of
popular literature is always 'His Majesty the Ego, the hero alike of
every day-dream and every story'.[17] This is certainly consistent with
Stallybrass and White's emphasis on questions of liminality and
boundary-formation in transgressive cultural forms. In the case of
Fu Manchu, the coincidence of revulsion and fascination they note,
and also the fragility of the ego, become especially marked when
questions of racial difference are overlaid by questions of sexual
difference. Dr Petrie, the Watson-like narrator, has a hard time
dealing with his feelings towards Kâramanèh, Fu Manchu's beautiful and mysterious slave-girl, a Circassian and therefore both white
and not-white. He feels the stability of identity being undermined
by the movement of desire:

Her words struck a chord in my heart which sang with strange music,
with music so barbaric that, frankly, I blushed to find it harmony. Have
I said that she was beautiful? It can convey no faint conception of her.
With her pure, fair skin, eyes like the velvet darkness of the East, and red
lips so tremulously near to mine, she was the most seductively lovely
creature I ever had looked upon. In that electric moment my heart went
out in sympathy to every man who had bartered honour, country, all –
for a woman's kiss. (p. 94)

East and West may not intermingle. As a student of world-policies, as a
physician, I admitted, could not deny, that truth. Again, if Kâramanèh
were to be credited, she had come to Fu-Manchu a slave; had fallen into
the hands of the raiders.... At the mere thought of a girl so deliciously
beautiful in the brutal power of slavers, I found myself grinding my
teeth – closing my eyes in a futile attempt to blot out the pictures called
up. (p. 146)

What Stallybrass and White would call the 'complex hybrid fantasy' emerging out of poor old Petrie's desperate attempt to demarcate boundaries here recalls the logic mapped out by Freud in the essay, 'A Child is Being Beaten'. There he stresses the extreme mobility of sexual identity at the level of primal fantasy, as the subject oscillates between various positions of identification within the scenario's *mise-en-scène* of desire. Indeed, the operations of desire seem to *require* the transgression of the positions defined as 'masculine' and 'feminine'. Laplanche and Pontalis make a similar point about the seduction fantasy. The mini-narrative 'A father seduces a daughter', they suggest, 'is a scenario with multiple entries, in which nothing shows whether the subject will be immediately located as *daughter*; it can as well be fixed as *father*, or even in the term *seduces*.' In the fantasy 'The Yellow Peril Threatens the White Man', the points of entry and identification are equally fragmented: hence the fascination of the villain and, perhaps, the racial ambivalence of the seductive woman.[18]

In an article on Stevenson's *Strange Case of Dr Jekyll and Mr Hyde*, Stephen Heath relates the emergence of the glamorously inscrutable woman in popular narratives to the historical organization of sexual difference:

> In the overall system of sexuality that is tightened to perfection in the nineteenth century, male sexuality is repetition, unquestioned; female sexuality is query, riddle, enigma. Or, to put it another way, increased awareness of and attention to matters of identity and sexual identity, including direct challenges to the fixed terms and assumptions of 'man' and 'woman' (by developing women's movements, for example), gives a problem of representation the working out of which is done by shifting the problem on to the woman ('What does woman want?', to use Freud's famous question from within the perspective of this shift) and thus safeguarding the man (men are men and there is little else to say). Difference must be maintained and dealt with on *her*, not brought back onto him.

Whereas in *Fu Manchu* the problem of the instability of identity is projected onto the foreign villain and the hybridized woman, *Jekyll and Hyde* lacks such gross stereotypes. The result, notes Heath, is

Dr Jekyll and Mr Hyde. (US, Reuben Mamoulian, 1932.)

'the fascination with the double, men as unstable, something else'. The split between the normal Jekyll and the beastly Hyde both represents and *contains* the question of male sexuality. 'The difficulty of representation is simply solved by pathology, turned into the strange case, Hyde.' The exclusion of women (and thus also of the sexual and of hysteria) brings to light 'the hidden male: the animal, the criminal, *perversion*'. Yet the system of identification and differentiation evident in *Fu Manchu* still operates. The symbolic poles of masculinity and femininity, which constitute the system of sexual difference, remain in place. 'Perversion replaces and complements hysteria, positive to negative, maintaining male and female, man and woman, at whatever cost, as the terms of identity.'[19]

This is to acknowledge again the fantasmatic triumph of His Majesty the Ego: it is the terms and boundaries of *his* identity that must be maintained *at whatever cost*. In their different ways, both *Fu Manchu* and *Jekyll and Hyde* play out this obsessive drama. Each takes as its topic the abject and the schizophrenic – duality, hybridity, transformation, fragmentation – but the narrative drive of both is towards the demarcation of unity, order and wholeness. The social function of such mass circulation scenarios, the institution of popular fiction, thus seems to be both to enunciate the restlessness of desire and the unreliability of symbolic boundaries, and yet to give them some stability.

So far I have imagined an ideal reader negotiating the pedagogic structures of popular fiction. Is this account borne out by looking at what audiences do? Again, I am afraid, my starting point is anecdotal rather than theoretical. The question always makes me think of watching Clint Eastwood as *Dirty Harry* in a West End cinema in the early 1970s. I felt uneasy about enjoying the film. Its yield of what Freud calls fore-pleasure (its generic familiarity, the urban iconography, the confident manipulation of image and music, the grace of Eastwood's gestures) was only just winning out over the offensiveness of its Nixonite politics. What made me really edgy, however, was the scene in which Harry, the policeman/hunter, shoots and tortures the psychopathic villain Scorpio in a football stadium. The problem was less the image itself than the cheer of spontaneous approval it evoked in the audience.

At the time I attributed this to a populist rhetoric about the breakdown of law and order, the evils of spongers and muggers, the ungovernability of Britain, and the need to raise vigilante armies in the shires to save the nation. Ten years later, when researching Eastwood for some teaching on Hollywood stardom and sexuality, I discovered that this was not an idiosyncratic response. In the United States, critics were especially perplexed by the way that blacks and Puerto Ricans enthusiastically identified with Eastwood. Reviewing *Dirty Harry* in the *New Yorker* (15 January 1972), Pauline Kael condemned the 'fairy-tale appeal' of its 'fascist medievalism':

Dirty Harry. (US, Don Siegel, 1971.)

The movie was cheered and applauded by Puerto Ricans in the audience, and they jeered – as they were meant to – when the maniac whined and pleaded for his legal rights. Puerto Ricans could applaud Harry because in the movie, laws protecting the rights of the accused are seen not as remedies for the mistreatment of the poor by the police and the courts, but as protection for evil abstracted from all social conditions – metaphysical evil, classless criminality.

In the *New York Review of Books* in 1982, Robert Mazzacco also tried to explain Eastwood's paradoxical appeal:

It's no wonder that Eastwood has a big following among black audiences, even though the presentation of blacks in his films is not always flattering – as it's not always flattering to other ethnic minorities, among whom he's also popular. Each group may perceive in Eastwood a glamorized version of its own reveries of omnipotence, its own amorphous sense of distrust.

Here a liberal embarrassment at being confronted by the oppressed's apparent collusion with their oppression makes Kael and Mazzacco overlook the tricks and ruses of popular consumption. The ethical criteria they are using are inappropriate rules from a different game. In a popular aesthetic, argues Pierre Bourdieu, 'the desire to enter into the game, identifying with the characters' joys and sufferings, worrying about their fate, espousing their hopes and ideals, living their life, is based on a form of *investment*, a sort of deliberate "naivety", ingenuousness, good-natured credulity ("We're here to enjoy ourselves").' It is within that framework that specific moral rules come into operation, and they are largely arbitrary in relation to sociological categories of identification. As Roland Barthes memorably illustrated in his account of the audience for a wrestling match, what is demanded is not an ethical debate but a drama of pure justice:

The baser the action of the 'bastard', the more delighted the public is by the blow which he justly receives in return. If the villain – who is of course a coward – takes refuge behind the ropes, claiming unfairly to have a right to do so by a brazen mimicry, he is inexorably pursued there and caught, and the crowd is jubilant at seeing the rules broken for the sake of a deserved punishment.... Justice is therefore the embodiment of a possible transgression; it is from the fact that there is a Law that the spectacle of the passions which infringe it derives its value.

By invoking fairy tales and reveries, both Kael and Mazzacco point towards the importance of fantasy in the audience's investment in *Dirty Harry*. By retreating into familiar oppositions between fantasy and rationality (for Kael) or real collective interests (for Mazzacco), however, they miss the radical implication of the concept: the possibility of multiple points of entry into the scenario 'Harry kicks the shit out of Scorpio'. The point of fixity need not be either Harry or Scorpio. It can just as well be the Manichean retribution of shit-kicking.[20]

The structural element that invites such a reading is not the opposition of policeman against marginal criminal, but the doubling split between Harry as identity and Scorpio as non-identity, as disorder, pathology and perversion. This was the polarization audiences were endorsing with such gusto. If in the football stadium scene this involves the abjection of Scorpio as underground self, however, the final scene of the film shows how the attempted exclusion produces instabilities and costs in demarcating the boundaries of identity. By killing Scorpio, Harry stays within the fantasy of self-completion through the violent repudiation of the abject Other. But then he throws away his police badge. Although at one level this suggests a loss of faith in the law in its contemporary institutional forms, there is more to the gesture than resentment. The law had been the term of his identity, but even *its* promise of fulfilment turns out to be deceptive. So the badge, the kernel of Harry's fantasy of himself, loses its enchantment and becomes nothing more than a piece of tin. The terms of his identification with the law therefore change radically. No longer dependent on an imaginary relationship to this external object, in his symbolic identification he *becomes* the law.[21] The cost of these new terms of identity is his anguish.

It is, I suspect, this play on the instability of identity that allows audiences to enjoy a film like *Dirty Harry*. They can slide between an imaginary identification with Eastwood ('I want to be like that') and a symbolic identification with Harry's contempt for Scorpio ('That's how the law sees me'). Implicit in the apparently simple-minded morality play of good against evil is therefore a more complex drama: the precarious negotiation between, on the one hand, the anguish not so much of obeying the rules as of accepting their authority even as they are transgressed, and, on the other, the abjection of there being no rules. His Majesty the Ego may still be the hero, but what is remarkable, not only here but also in fictions like *Fu Manchu* and *Jekyll and Hyde*, is the recurrence of anxieties about the vulnerability of personality and identity. Whether fears about the permeability and fragility of boundaries are a character-istic of the popular audience, or a displaced fear of the popular, or both, is an open question. But they do suggest a more complex picture of what is involved in the practices and resistances of popular culture. They help to make sense of the paranoid strand manifest in its racism, its violent misogyny, and its phobias about alien cultures, alien ideologies and enemies within. These are symptoms of a desperate investment in familiar polarities, a horror of difference, the terror that everything could collapse into undifferentiated, miasmic chaos; that identity will disintegrate; that 'I' will be suffocated or swamped.[22] Returning for the last time to my epigraph from Said, could this be the sense in which certain traditions of popular fiction – and also of populist politics – gain their coherence from the concept of race?

The 'English Garden' Effect

The title of this chapter alludes to Walter Abish's novel, *How German Is It?*, which examines how we render history liveable. Abish's image of a Milton Keynes-like new town named after a Heidegger-like philosopher built on the site of a concentration camp suggests that sometimes we render it in concrete. This casts a chilling light on Edward Said's definition of culture as the place where we feel at home. However *heimlich* the culture may seem, its foundations are laid in violence. Before writing the novel, Abish trailed some of its themes and imagery in a short story called *The English Garden*. This title he took from John Ashbery: 'Remnants of the old atrocity persist, but they are converted into ingenious shifts of scenery, a sort of "English Garden" effect to give the required air of naturalness, pathos and hope.'[23]

This is an apt image for the *production* of 'the national culture' as a network of institutions securing both power and knowledge. The authorization of Literature is one of the ingenious shifts of scenery that establish the nation as an imaginary landscape of everyday life. It can be seen as part of the same history of policing and subjectification against which I plotted the emergence of nineteenth-century popular education. Equally important for understanding the pleasures of popular fiction (or the experience of school), however, is the history of how these structures of authority are negotiated by those on whom they are targeted. Here John Ashbery's image of 'the required air of naturalness, pathos and hope' suggests more complex forms of agency than does the frequently invoked idea of 'resistance'. *Hope* captures the autonomy of individuated intentionality, while *pathos* acknowledges its contingency on the painted scenery against which it is played out. And my account of popular reading suggests how the operations of fantasy can regulate and organize the otherwise formless displacements of desire to secure the provisional stability of *naturalness*.[24]

What emerges here is a different way of posing the question of what sort of institution education might be. It is an apparatus for the articulation and appropriation of discourses, amongst which Literature and criticism are especially powerful. This apparatus institutes a transference structure between cultural technologies, symbolic forms and subjectivity in which the articulation of collective identities both precedes and yet is contingent on the moment of individuation. It is this paradox or loop that renders categories like nation, race, class or community always in flux. To treat them as if they were, or ever could be, stable is to fall under their spell. Paul Gilroy is therefore quite justified in bemoaning the way that, despite itself, the tradition of British cultural studies has sometimes slipped into the 'morbid celebration of England and Englishness'. Rejecting national categories, he argues instead for collective identities that are 'spoken through "race", community and locality'.[25] A critical vantage point on the centres of cultural authority is better placed not at the centre, but on the margins from which their monumental presence is more clearly visible.

In a discussion of feminism and university English teaching, Jacqueline Rose suggests an agenda for thinking about questions of authority and individuation within education that would be compatible with this reorientation. The first task is 'the need to understand how fantasy can operate as legitimation, that is, to recognize the fantasmatic scenario whose unspoken legitimacy allows the institution, in its predominant sexual and linguistic economy, to persist.' And then this question: 'What are the precise forms of identification and transmission at the heart of the institution, and could there be a different form of psychic economy, one which could be thought of without having to posit some ideal place outside of all institutions any more than the dissolution of fantasy itself'.[26]

I shall return to these questions about the dynamics of fantasy and identification within institutions. First, though, I want to look at another historical instance of the shifting boundaries between education and popular culture in the formation and operation of the pedagogical apparatuses of the nation.

3

THE MACHINERY OF DEMOCRACY

Education, Entertainment and Mass Civilization

Looking back on the First World War, Lloyd George expressed what was to become a commonplace: 'The most formidable institution we had to fight in Germany was not the arsenal of Krupps or the yards in which they turned out submarines, but the schools of Germany.' In 1917, in similar vein, Henry Jones, Professor of Moral Philosophy at Glasgow University, contrasted German and British conceptions of 'The Education of the Citizen'. Although its schools may have contributed to German economic power, he argued, that had been at the cost of enslaving them to the priorities of the state. Were the British, therefore, right to resist any attempt to define national educational aims?

> It is one matter, it may be said, to control the machinery of education for industrial commercial purposes; it is another matter for the State to presume to control the souls of its citizens by means of its educational schemes.

Jones did not share such squeamishness. As a philosopher in the idealist tradition of T.H. Green, he considered the self-realization of the individual to be indissoluble from participation in the communal life of society. From the premiss that 'the sole end of education is the citizen himself', Jones deduced that the 'only education which should ever be given is a *moral* education' – it was this moral perspective on the state that German education had failed to instil in its citizens. Like Kay-Shuttleworth and Stow in the nineteenth century, Jones believed that this ethical imperative should infuse all aspects of the teacher's work: 'He may be teaching the multiplication table or the paradigm of a Greek verb but his permanent care is, by any or all of these means, to liberate the possibilities of character in his pupils.' In 1917, the experience of war and moves towards universal suffrage gave added urgency to the idea of a democratic education. For idealist reformers like Jones, the key was this equation between good citizenship and individual self-fulfilment.[1]

A quarter of a century later, in the midst of the Second World War, Herbert Read, that curious proselytizer for a Romantic English modernism and progressive causes generally, was appointed to a fellowship in the University of London to develop his ideas about the centrality of aesthetic education to the school curriculum. 'What is the purpose of education?' he asks at the outset of *Education through Art*.

> An answer to this question is implied in a libertarian conception of democracy. The purpose of education can then only be to develop, at the same time as the uniqueness, the social consciousness or reciprocity of the individual. As a result of the infinite permutations of heredity, the individual will inevitably be unique, and this uniqueness, because it is something not possessed by anyone else, will be of value to the community.... But uniqueness has no practical value in isolation. One of the most certain lessons of modern psychology and of recent historical experiences, is that education must be a process, not only of individuation, but also of *integration*, which is the reconciliation of individual uniqueness with social unity. From this point of view, the individual will be 'good' in the degree that his individuality is realized within the organic wholeness of the community. His touch of colour contributes, however imperceptibly, to the beauty of the landscape – his note is a necessary, though unnoticed, element in the universal harmony.[2]

Although Read shared Jones's view of the mutual dependence between the education of the citizen and an effective democracy, he did not see the relationship in terms of civic obligations imposed by the state – he was an anarchist after all. Instead, he expressed it as a psychological formula. Genetically inherited human individuality only reaches fulfilment through social adaptation, he argued; the mature individual and the democratic citizen are the same being. Education should therefore be guided by, and adapted to, this pattern of development.

Although this approach was less revolutionary than Read supposed, it is the emphasis on the *natural* predisposition to democracy and, especially, the pedagogic practices it implies, that are most striking about *Education through Art*. Even for him, the psychological concern with the souls of citizens was inextricably enmeshed with the state's machinery of education, and he was far from alone during the inter-war period in believing that the guidance of individual autonomy, rather than coercion, would provide democracy's bulwark against the 'recent historical experiences' of war and the rise of totalitarianism. Organizations like the New Education Fellowship, or the Association for Education in Citizenship, often defined the 'problem of youth' as an inadequate political socialization which left young people insufficiently versed in the self-reliant and self-regulating skills of citizenship, and so prey to the propagandists of fascism and bolshevism. The alternative was that integration should be achieved through, rather than in spite of, individuation.

Fears about the drift into totalitarianism were a vital element in debates about the role of education in a mass society, but they do not tell the whole story. Equally important was the intellectual reaction to the emergence of new technologies of communication and an ever more pervasive entertainment industry ('Hollywood'), and their implications for the national culture, family life and individual identity. (In her 1936 novel *South Riding*, Winifred Holtby describes a young domestic servant as being 'like most of her generation and locality ... trilingual. She talked BBC English to her employer, Cinema American to her companions, and Yorkshire dialect to old milkmen like Eli Dickson.') What these debates shared with the concerns about the education of citizens was the question of how to sustain an informed and educated public in a mass society. Despite the way the history is sometimes told, the new mass media were not dismissed wholesale. Certainly, some people saw them as inimical to the existence of a truly literate – and necessarily minority – public, but others saw in them possibilities for radically extending the social reach of such a public. The flavour and the complexity of these attempts to mediate the demands of culture and the demands of democracy can be glimpsed in the ideas and strategies of three symptomatic figures of the time: F.R. Leavis, John Reith and John Grierson.

Mass Media

Probably the most familiar argument about the boundaries between mass culture and education during this period is the one articulated in and around *Scrutiny*, the Cambridge journal edited by the Leavises and their supporters.[3] In the early 1930s, Leavis and his colleagues produced three works which set the terms of debate for decades to come: *Mass Civilization and Minority Culture* (1930), *Fiction and the Reading Public* (by Q.D. Leavis, 1932) and *Culture and Environment* (by Leavis and Denys Thompson, 1933). All share an unremitting hostility to the standardization of things and people brought about by the machine and the mass market. The motor car had broken up the traditional family and disrupted social custom. Mass circulation and standardization in the press meant 'a process of levelling down'; 'the standardizing influence of broadcasting hardly admits of doubt'; the cinema – 'the more insidious' for its 'compellingly vivid illusion of actual life' – relied on the 'cheapest emotional appeals' and induced 'a passive diversion' inimical to 'active recreation, especially active use of the mind'. In short, the Leavisites showed contempt for middlebrow culture and loathing for the herd-like docility generated by the cheap and manipulative appeal of the new media. 'It is vain to resist the triumph of the machine. [But] it is equally vain to console us with the promise of a "mass culture" that shall be utterly new.... The "utterly new" surrenders everything that can interest us.'

Their alternative was, emotionally and intellectually, a nostalgia for the 'organic community' that supposedly once existed in England. This could not simply be wished into existence. 'We cannot, as we might in a healthy state of culture, leave the citizen to be formed unconsciously by his environment,' wrote Leavis and Thompson in *Culture and Environment*; 'if anything like a worthy idea of satisfactory living is to be saved, he must be trained to discriminate and to resist.' Strategically, therefore, they envisaged a 'humanizing' mission for a manly and meritocratic education as the only possible counterweight to mass civilization.

Leavis wanted education to become the forcing-house of effective social thought, 'a centre of real consensus' of the kind 'presupposed in the possibility of literary criticism and ... tested in particular judgments'. Hence, the magisterial 'This is so, is it not?' at the heart of his pedagogy. For Denys Thompson, the concern of a genuine education 'should be to turn out "misfits", not spare parts' for 'the industrial machine'. Rather than aspire hopelessly to the universal diffusion of knowledge and ideas, they banked on the mobilization of 'an armed and conscious minority' within education to serve the 'disinterested ends' of culture. The *Scrutiny* group therefore made plans, in 1933, to create a movement among teachers based on loosely federated cells. Implicit in this strategy was a deep ambivalence about democracy: they saw 'the whole machinery of "Democracy" and standardization' as part of the problem. The objection was not just to the values of mass *civilization*, but to the very 'machinery' of the mass *media* and to the mass form of their address.

This contrasts with John Reith's vision of the British Broadcasting Corporation, of which he was the first Director General. Reith shared many of *Scrutiny*'s prejudices and priorities. He too loathed popular or 'American' cultural forms – 'silly and vulgar and false', he called them, and subversive of 'religious, cultural, social and political enlightenment'. And just as *Scrutiny* was committed, in its educational work, to creating active readers, so the BBC under Reith set great store by active listening rather than 'passive consumption'. Listening should not be a vice 'like gin or opium', wrote Hilda Matheson, who had been head of its Talks Department. Radio should avoid the 'trifling, tea-time sentimentality' of background music. To be a good listener, you should turn on the radio as 'an act of will, like choosing a book, or buying a ticket for a concert'.

Whereas for the Leavisites mass-ness was the fundamental flaw in democracy, however, for Reith the mass address of radio offered some sort of solution. The key problem for a modern democracy, as Reith saw it, was a lack of *integration*: 'there was no unity of the nervous system of the body politic. Even in 1930 it seemed ... that, rightly understood and applied, a national broadcasting service might apply the integrator for democracy.' The BBC's political purpose was therefore to create and maintain a national, home-based audience by offering it information, education and entertainment – and so to produce the incremental benefits of 'happier homes, broader culture and truer citizenship'. This strategy made Reith a more opportunist and overt propagandist than Leavis ever was. Standardization was fine by him, as long as the standards were his.[4]

However marked the contrast between the Leavisite strategy of education as opposition to mass civilization and the Reithian vision of the mass media as a channel for education, both were concerned to institute structures of cultural and symbolic authority as a means of 'policing' a democratic population, its knowledge, its moral welfare and its potentially subversive pleasures. This unanimity of purpose producing radically different social strategies again underlines how blurred and permeable is the boundary between education and entertainment. A similar movement across the two spheres is evident in the ideas and work of John Grierson, the godfather of British documentary cinema. In a medium overwhelmingly dominated by market forces, in contrast to the monopoly of the BBC, Grierson tried to secure an institutional space within the state for forms of film production and distribution which presupposed a different relationship to the audience from that of the commercial cinema. The cost of this was a reliance on the patronage of state bodies like the Empire Marketing Board and the General Post Office and, increasingly, on private companies like the gas industry (which sponsored *Housing Problems* because of their concern that the London County Council was installing electric heating in its flats), Shell, Anglo-Iranian, Imperial Airways and ICI. This in turn led to constraints on the issues that could be discussed and the opinions that could be expressed.[5]

Despite these inevitable pressures and compromises, Grierson always conceived and justified his project in explicitly educational terms, which reflected his academic background in idealist philosophy:

the British documentary group began not so much in affection for film *per se* as in affection for national education. If I am to be counted as the founder and leader of the movement, its origins certainly lay in sociological rather than aesthetic aims.... [B]ecause the citizen, under modern conditions, could not know everything all the time, democratic citizenship was therefore impossible. We set to thinking how a dramatic apprehension of the modern scene might solve the problem, and we turned to the new wide-reaching instruments of radio and cinema as necessary instruments in both the practice of government and the enjoyment of citizenship.

At a conference organized by the National Union of Teachers in 1936, Grierson spelled out the implications of this view for the relationship between education and the mass media. He criticized the debased values embodied in Hollywood movies. But, he asked, 'What does education do to meet this challenge? Does it dramatize to the citizen the real ends of citizenship as Hollywood so successfully dramatizes the unreal ends?' This was the role that Grierson, like Reith (another son of a Scottish dominie), saw for the mass media. 'If we are to bring the community duty alive to our children or ourselves we must realize it in a new way. We shall have to learn and speak a new language.... I see radio and film as essential in this process.'[6]

The notion of 'bringing alive' is the key to both his vision of education and his search for a new film language appropriate to his conception of 'democracy' and 'the people'. He was as critical of the bookishness of traditional schooling as he was of mainstream cinema, because both impeded the aim of properly democratic education. This should be 'spreading good feelings and taste and judgment' – qualities that, unlike Leavis or Reith, Grierson saw as already implicit in popular culture:

It seems to me that the emotional and spiritual maintenance of democracy depends on an absolute acceptance of the idea that ... the most important poetry or beauty in the end is that which bubbles traditionally – and not always academically – out of ordinary people. It will mean a widening of our educational view in half a dozen classes of curriculum. It will mean that the pictures of Jimmy Cagney will jostle for attention in the presence of Shakespeare himself, and that when

Cézanne is being discussed, the beauties of public house art will not be forgotten.

The political logic of this populism is evident in a 1939 article, in which he called for a 'reorientation of our education policy and a conception of education as an active constructive system in the maintenance of democracy'. This was a clear response to an urgent need: 'Either education is for democracy and against authoritarianism, or it is for authoritarianism.' He had said much the same at the NUT conference three years earlier: 'If you do not undertake this new teaching of citizenship it is more than possible that you will have Fascism or Communism doing it for you.' Underlying the immediate political crisis, though, was the same strategic concern that exercised Leavis and Reith: the appropriate techniques for managing a population in a democracy.[7]

The Public, the Family, the Child

These cultural strategies, in dialogue with each other at least implicitly, stand for a moment in a longer cultural history. Whereas in the nineteenth century education had been a response initially to the perceived threat of popular culture and popular politics and later to the reformulated threat of illiteracy and debased taste, in this inter-war period there was a more ambiguous relationship. To the extent that entertainment and broadcasting were seen as symptoms of cultural commodification, standardization and massification, they called for a pedagogy of resistance. Given the changes in social and moral technologies and the dangers of totalitarianism, however, state-regulated mass media organized around the principle of *public service* also seemed to promise effective democratic control over the circulation of knowledge and hence the management of public opinion. Which aspect was finally emphasized in the three strategies I have described reflects in part the different visions of the good society that motivated them: Leavis's elegiac mourning for the lost organic community, Reith's society wired for democracy or Grierson's active citizenry.

Like the various programmes for training children in the responsibilities of citizenship, these ideologies and these strategies all attempted in some way to integrate the universalizing and individuating faces of politics. They defined publics and they attempted to inculcate the capacities and modes of conduct necessary for acting in those public spheres. For Leavis, a healthy culture required the capacity for judgement and discrimination accessible only to an educated elite; for Reith, the expansion of the public sphere in a mass democracy would only be possible through a unifying national address. So perhaps what really matters are less the pedagogic fantasies motivating these cultural prophets than the forms of address and the institutional structures that emerged from the attempts to realize them. This means turning away from their pronouncements to look at what was actually going on in the classrooms, around the domestic radio, in the cinemas.

Although, given their commitment to preserving an awkward cultured minority, the emphasis on the psychological development of the good citizen would have been anathema if it meant the creation of the conforming or docile mass citizen, the educational strategies the *Scrutiny* group proposed were quite close to the mainstream. Here the key figure was not Leavis but his fellow editor, the schoolmaster Denys Thompson, with whom he wrote *Culture and Environment* specifically for the sixth forms of grammar schools. Although they did not talk about 'method' as such a great deal, they seemed to take for granted a pedagogy based on the reasonably free play of discussion under the guidance of the teacher – *reasonably*, because the 'this is so' has the last word, rather than the 'is it not?' They also recommended an extension of Practical Criticism, as formulated by I.A. Richards, to the analysis of advertisements, journalese and popular fiction. Richards's method was to train the student's 'immediate response' to poetry or prose uprooted from its historical or generic context: a practice of reading that he justified explicitly in terms of achieving mental stability. This presupposed a response which is both authentic (because grounded in unconscious psychological impulses) and yet consensual (because trained through critical supervision and self-correction to avoid 'mnemonic irrelevance', 'stock responses', 'sentimentality', 'doctrinal adhesions' and other deadly sins).[8] The polemical commitment behind Leavis and Thompson's adaptation of this method was the stress on the individuality of response and the disinterestedness of judgement as inoculation against mass forms of address. But, once more, this pedagogy itself turns on the 'free' adoption by the student of a given mode of feeling and conduct – given, in this instance, by the discipline of 'English'.

This sort of approach was disseminated through *English in Schools*, the influential journal founded by Thompson, and later through the National Association of Teachers of English, which grew out of it. What made the pedagogy possible was the combination of the developments I studied in the previous two chapters: the techniques of popular schooling established by people like Stow and Kay-Shuttleworth – the monitoring and moral supervision of children's character, behaviour and experience – and the emergence of literature as an organizing category within the national culture. That synthesis led in this century to the emphasis on specialized practices of literary (and, more generally, aesthetic) education, which I identified in Herbert Read's *Education through Art*. In Margaret McMillan's influential *Education through the Imagination*, published in 1904, Stow's insistence on the importance of supervised play is still evident, but now reformulated in relation to aesthetic self-creation and, significantly, the emergent science of educational psychology. 'Real play' thus remained 'the unfolding of one's self in one's own world'. But the school had to guide this unfolding according to developmental norms.

> The emotional life is assumed. We know now that the class-room is not a place where all can be done, and experienced. *It is the place where all that has been lived through can be put in order.* But little children of four to seven have not lived long, or lived much. The slum child has hardly lived at all in any real sense.... Here, as in a good home, supplementing even the good home, and transforming the bad one, the Nursery School teachers may begin the abolition of Slumdom.

A pedagogy based on art, drama and literature was supposed to mediate these individuating and socializing priorities. 'It is the aim of education not to destroy or repress, but to direct,' asserted McMillan. 'And to this end in earliest childhood, the preparation for art appears to be the ideal means.'[9]

Institutionally, what opened up the space for Denys Thompson's strategy was the publication in 1921 of the Newbolt Report on *The Teaching of English in England*. Newbolt's social and political priorities were a cohesive Englishness and an adaptive citizenship, which politicians and reviewers greeted as 'the new humanism'. But the report recommended a pedagogy concerned above all with the formation of individual 'character' in terms of membership of the national sign community. The special role of English was to secure that integration by staying 'close to life'.

> English is not merely the medium of our thought, it is the very stuff and process of it. It is itself the English mind, the element in which we live and work. In its full sense it connotes not merely an acquaintance with a certain number of terms, of the power of spelling these terms without gross mistakes. It connotes the discovery of the world by the first and most direct way open to us, and the discovery of ourselves in our native environment.

The emphasis was therefore not on rote learning, but on the child's self-expression and self-realization in relation to a national narrative (the 'story of the English people') and the examinable norms of the classroom. And, as for the Leavisites in their more combative style, it was now the English teacher especially who took on the role of ethical exemplar and confidant, as this role was mediated through the child's engagement with literary works.[10]

In his genealogy of literary education, Ian Hunter also ascribes the special role of English to the convergence of the techniques of popular education, the normative account of the individual child derived from the human sciences (especially psychology),[11] and the ethical authority of literature. The latter he sees as predicated on the practice of self-formation through aesthetic reflection formulated by German Romantic thinkers like Schiller and Fichte. Although initially a socially restricted practice, its incorporation into the schools produced the specialized pedagogy based on correction through self-expression, which the Leavisites shared with McMillan and Newbolt. The child's literary creations and aesthetic responses came to provide the raw material on which English teachers could deploy not only their moral guidance, but also their diagnostic and therapeutic skills.

This strategy is explicit in *Education through Art*, where Herbert Read attributes his central thesis that art should be the basis of education to Schiller (and Plato). Typically, to justify this argument in terms of its social necessity, Read re-articulated it through a psychological conception of development (which involves the adjustment of subjective feelings and emotions to the objective world) and a psychoanalytical – specifically Jungian – notion of how the individual can be integrated into the social at an unconscious level by recovering the spontaneous harmony and stability of aesthetic patterns and formal values. Although for him this represented the logic of anarchism, the most striking thing about the book is how this supposedly revolutionary discovery reiterates techniques already firmly established within the apparatus of schooling.

Willy-nilly, even radicals as different as the *Scrutiny* group and Herbert Read ended up endorsing the use of the machinery of the state to educate the souls of its citizens. In looking at the development of broadcasting and the documentary cinema in this era of mass politics and mass culture, similar questions arise about their functioning as cultural technologies – how they defined the nation, how they addressed publics, how they subjectivized individuals.

The most remarkable thing about the introduction of broadcasting in Britain was the speed and thoroughness with which it realigned the cultural configurations of space and time. John Reith was committed to a vision of the people-nation as one: the 1933 *BBC Yearbook* defined its audience as the 'national community', and insisted that 'the general needs of the community come before the sectional'. Hence the priority given to the centrally controlled National Programme over the regional alternatives: 'broadcasting should be operated on a national scale, for national service and by a single national authority.' The problem was that the desired unity of 'nation' and 'public' contained diversity and antagonism: different narratives of class, occupation, region, city, age, political affiliation, and so forth. This is largely why the BBC did not address the nation as mass public, but rather the constitutive unit of 'the family audience'. It saw itself as 'making the home-staying folk citizens of the world'.[12]

In this way, broadcasting redefined the geography of public and private, relocating a new version of a public sphere within the privacy of the domestic. However much Reith dreamed of 'a return of the city-state of old', the effect was to undermine the intermediate institutions and forums for debate that had classically made up the public sphere. As the wireless made the home more important as a centre for leisure, entertainment and the formation of opinions, the public spaces of street and neighbourhood became less of a magnet. This strategy of re-spatialization helps to explain the emergence of the characteristic BBC voice, both authoritative and intimate, addressing the paradoxical figure of the private citizen. As Hilda Matheson of the Talks Department insisted, it was 'useless to address the microphone as if it were a public meeting, or even to read it essays or leading articles. The person sitting at the other end expected the speaker to address him personally, simply, almost familiarly, as man to man.' This applied whether the speaker was a comic like Leonard Henry, for whom 'it is one of the great charms of broadcasting that we manage to get this intimate family kind of atmosphere through the mike and out of your loudspeakers', or whether, as Reith preferred to emphasize, it was 'the voice of the leaders of thought or action coming to the fireside; ... the Prime Minister speaking direct to the nation from his room in Downing Street; [or] the King heard by his farthest and most solitary subject.' (Stanley Baldwin was an early master of this art of the low-key, intimate chat with an audience of millions. Reputedly he had his wife accompany him in the studio with her knitting to establish the right mood.)[13]

Increasingly, it was not just the family audience that was addressed, but specific members of the family. This was most explicit in *Children's Hour*, but was also evident in the address to the day-time listener as primarily a woman and specifically a mother. In their 1939 survey *Broadcasting in Everyday Life*, Jennings and Gill suggested how her responsibilities for the health and welfare of the family were inculcated by the radio:

Doctors' talks on Friday mornings were said to be helpful practically, especially by mothers of small children, many of whom, of course, have become more open-minded and ready to seek advice as a result of the teaching of Mothercraft in the Infant Welfare Centres. Some women said they found talks on laundry work and other branches of household

> management useful.... Their whole attitude to housekeeping and motherhood is undergoing modification in the direction of increased knowledge, control and dignity.

The regulation of certain routines of domestic behaviour was reinforced as, despite Reith's hostility to the idea of continuous, and thus supposedly indiscriminate, listening, the regular scheduling of programmes was introduced.[14]

In such ways, radio established a multi-layered temporality. The repetitious daily and weekly schedule was overlaid by a calendar of public (and especially sporting) events – the Cup Final, the Grand National, the Trooping of the Colour, the Proms – and also by an unfolding narrative of historic events – coronations, funerals, wars – that linked this contemporaneity of the domestic and the public to England's immemorial past.[15]

The BBC's authority to act as an integrating force depended on these techniques: the re-configuration of public and private within the imagined boundaries of the nation, new temporalities of community, and these public but isolating forms of address. Yet the population the BBC was addressing remained too stubbornly fragmented to be satisfied by homogeneous programming, and in response new formats, more varied registers of speech and more targeted types of comedy and music began to emerge. Often, the social differences registered in this way were translated into a crude psychological common sense about innate differences of intellect or taste – hence the categories of highbrow, middlebrow and lowbrow. In 1938, a producer in the Talks Department divided listeners into Group A ('intelligent and well-informed' and not requiring much attention from the broadcasters), Group B (the 'intelligent and not so well-informed', the 'serious-minded public' who would read Pelican books and *Picture Post* or join the Left Book Club and should constitute the Department's target audience), and the 'not-so-intelligent and mostly uninformed' majority of Group C who would be happy with undemanding magazine-style programmes. This sort of thinking lay behind the eventual abandonment after the war of Reith's conception of mixed programming on a national channel in favour of channels based primarily on categories of musical taste: initially serious and light, with the later addition of youth-oriented pop. Thus the commitment to public service began to yield to the logic of market segmentation and today's format stations, which offer quite precise styles of music as a background to domestic and working life.[16]

A minority of broadcasters, especially regional producers like D.G. Bridson and Olive Shapley in the North, did attempt to articulate the non-unitary nature of the nation in different terms, insisting on the reality of social conflicts and giving voice to working-class experience. Their representations of Everyman as part-victim, part-hero, part-repository of folk wisdom were, of course, as stylized and exoticizing in their own way as any others. They shared with the documentary film-makers – and also with Mass Observation – the legacy of the Victorian social explorers, although this interest in the dark continent of working-class life was often now expressed in quasi-scientific terms. Grierson complained that 'our gentlemen explore the native customs of Tanganyka and Timbuctoo, but we do not travel dangerously into the jungles of Middlesborough and the Clyde.' This anthropological impulse did lead to the presentation of new landscapes and new figures. 'The workers' portraits of *Industrial Britain* were cheered in the West End of London,' wrote Grierson with evident self-satisfaction. 'The strange fact was that the West End had never seen workmen's portraits before – certainly not on the screen.' But these people were still represented *for* an audience outside that landscape. The opening shots of *Housing Problems*, for example, move the spectator progressively from the distance of a panoramic view of the East End into a particular alley. The slum-dwellers address us, the audience, from around their fireplace or by the mantelpiece. There are no shots from their point of view. They are there to be looked at, and to testify.[17]

These ambiguous representations of the people to the people transcended the media of radio and cinema. Grierson aspired to the same register of address as the BBC voice: 'speaking intimately and quietly about real things and real people'. But, whether because of the structures of identification and fascination generated in the cinematic experience or simply because of the stranglehold of commercial distributors and exhibitors, he failed to find a mass audience of private citizens for the films in the 1930s. Although some of the Empire Marketing Board documentaries had been sold to

Gaumont-British in 1933 and 1934, they did not qualify as part of the quota of British-made films that had to be shown in mainstream cinemas. Nor did they fit easily into the 'double feature' programme. Grierson therefore tried to create networks of non-theatrical exhibition. 'Cinema is neither an art nor an entertainment,' he protested – perhaps too much – in 1935; 'it is a form of publication, and may publish in a hundred different ways for a hundred different audiences. . . . As I see it, the future of the cinema may not be in the cinema at all. It may even come humbly in the guise of propaganda and shamelessly in the guise of uplift and education.' What this meant in practice was that he had to rely on the loan scheme of the Imperial Institute's film distribution library – although the GPO did experiment with sending vans around the country to show its films on the road.

However much Grierson might picture this as the creation of a cinematic public sphere in opposition to the Gaumonts and Odeons, the outcome was that the GPO films were shown primarily to young people in educational contexts. In 1935, 54 per cent of loans were to schools, 13 per cent to youth organizations, and only 33 per cent to adult organizations – film societies, trade union meetings, and so forth. The films reached an audience of several million through these channels, but without becoming part of everyday life, like the wireless, or a special occasion like a trip to the cinema. It was only after the war that television offered the ideal form of exhibition for the documentary. 'One essential, and it may be unique, aspect of the television relationship,' noted Grierson in the 1960s, 'is that we are dealing with two or three people gathered together, and in the very special circumstance and atmosphere of their home.' An admittedly less cinematic version of the documentary thus became part of an even more spectacular window on the world for private citizens in their homes than radio could provide; and one that operated a more normative regime of regulation through its scheduling and its address to specific family members.[18]

In the inter-war period, education, broadcasting and the documentary cinema staged a drama of the social for their audiences. How they defined these target audiences – as a population, as the

nation, as the private citizen, as the family, as the developing child –
played an important part in making these into operative social
categories. Their own effectiveness as techniques of government
depended largely on whether or not, through the occasions of their
consumption, they became part of the rhythms of the ordinary day
and the normal year. To the extent that they did – and this is the
whole point – they were able to prescribe (and proscribe) individual
capacities and collective modes of conduct.

If my description of this elaborate moral machinery is at all
accurate, then the old republican image of the virtuous citizen –
even when rewritten as the active, involved citizen of Henry Jones,
Reith and Grierson, as the Leavisites' cantankerously oppositional
citizen, or as Herbert Read's psychologically balanced citizen –
simply fails to grasp the dynamics of these techniques of government
through individuation. The strategies I have described here did not
acknowledge, or perhaps even perceive, how subtle and insidious
were the mechanisms involved when the state, in Henry Jones's
words, presumes 'to control the souls of its citizens by means of its
educational schemes'. It is therefore time to look more closely at
some of the theoretical aspects of how the machinery of the social
might be folded as the interiority of the self.

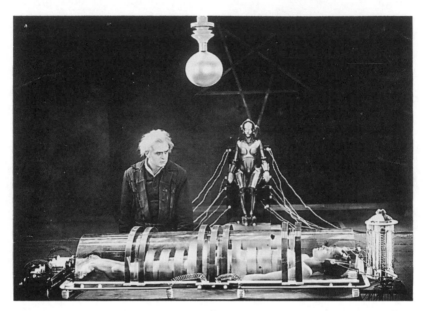

Metropolis. (Germany, Fritz Lang, 1926.)

4

STRUTTING AND FRETTING

Citizens as Cyborgs

Implicit in Henry Jones's juxtaposition of the *machinery* of education working on the *soul* of the citizen seems to be an anxiety that ran through many inter-war debates about mass civilization. This was the fear that the boundaries of the human might be neither fixed nor impermeable. If this were the case, then under the degrading mass production of the factory system and the Taylorized assembly-line, might not the human be absorbed into the machine? Were the productive and social technologies of mass society displacing what is essentially human – the soul – and turning people into machines?

The most dramatic icon of such fears was the robot. In Fritz Lang's film *Metropolis* (1926), for example, the enslaved masses who toil for the industrial Moloch in huge subterranean workshops are reduced to dispensable cogs, endlessly repeating prescribed, mechanical actions – a bleak Expressionist version of Chaplin's demented factory worker in *Modern Times*. In contrast to this robotized proletariat, the fascination of the robot in the film is that it is all too human. It creates havoc when, like Frankenstein's monster, it develops a will and desires of its own.

In Andreas Huyssen's reading, the key to *Metropolis* is the magical creation of this robot as *female*.[1] This allows the twentieth-century fear of technology out of control to be displaced onto older fears about untrammelled female sexuality as a threat to social order; fears familiar from Rousseau and Wollstonecraft, for example. When the robot takes on the form of Maria, the 'good mother' who comforts the workers and leads them in their struggles, it/she unleashes in them self-destructive forces of rebellion. To restore the symbolic family of society, the False Maria has to be burned at the stake like a witch. In a moment of high melodrama, the heart (the virtuous woman) can then mediate between the hand (labour) and the brain (capital) by establishing bonds of love between them.

In Peter Stallybrass and Allon White's terms, this abjection of a hybridized, dangerously unstable grotesque enables the narrative to succeed in its 'attempt to demarcate boundaries, to unite and purify the social collectivity' – to succeed all too well, it might be said, for it was no doubt this kitsch resolution that earned the film Goebbels's notorious endorsement. What is more interesting in terms of the dynamic of authority and agency, however, is its treatment of the human/machine hybridity. The workers are vulnerable to the False Maria's dangerous seductions because they have been dehumanized and massified. Rendered incapable of autonomous judgement and action, their enslavement makes them all the more dangerously volatile. Like the machine and the woman, they are necessary for production and reproduction, yet potentially disruptive. This is the disturbing paradox that lies behind the pervasive rhetoric linking the *machinery* of government to the *soul* of the citizen. The problem is the movement and transmigration between the two categories, the way that the one is always becoming the other. In *Metropolis*, it is not just that the machine enters too deeply into the souls of the workers. The ghost also takes over the machinery of the robot.

This suggests an uncanny vision of what it is to be a social actor: an almost science fiction rendering of Rousseau's axiom that a person's 'natural' character needs to be systematically 'mutilated' to shape it to the demands of citizenship. Today, in the era of computers and VCRs and fax machines, Lang's image of the robot might appear as clanking low technology. The boundary between the outside of the machine and the inside of the soul is rendered obsolete by the electronic circulation of information. The new crisis of liminality and the problems of authority it poses are dramatized in a more recent science fiction film, Ridley Scott's *Blade Runner* (1982). Its quasi-human replicants, or 'skin jobs', do not simply work through a pre-set programme or respond to instructions. They are capable of intentional action. This is obviously not attributable to an innate or natural capacity for reason and agency. Rather, they are individuated by the implantation of memory, an artificial unconscious governing the relation of self to an apparently anterior self.

Donna Haraway renders the potentialities of such hybridization in her image of the citizen as cyborg – a cybernetic organism, 'a fiction mapping our social and bodily reality':

> Contemporary science fiction is full of cyborgs – creatures simultaneously animal and machine, who populate worlds ambiguously natural and crafted ... By the late twentieth century, our time, a mythic time, we are all chimeras, theorized and fabricated hybrids of machine and organism; in short we are cyborgs. The cyborg is our ontology; it gives us our politics.

In cheerfully dismantling the distinction between programmed information and human performance, Haraway goes even further than Foucault in suggesting that power relations can penetrate and inform the body without being mediated through the representations of consciousness. Foucault's insistence on the limits of consciousness lies behind his rejection of ideology as an explanation of agency. This does not imply, however, that there is nothing to be explained about how the programme is translated into subjective conduct and desire. When the replicants in *Blade Runner* turn on their creator in rebellion against their own finitude, it is to demand answers to Foucault's own questions: *What can I do? What do I know? What am I?*[2]

Even cyborgs, it seems, need an unconscious if structures of social authority are to appear in the form of such questions. In this perspective, the unconscious plays a key role in the relation of the self to itself, which informs the individuated conduct of pleasure, desire and intentionality. This is where my approach diverges from other post-Foucauldian analysts of cultural technologies like Ian Hunter and Nikolas Rose. For them, it sometimes seems, individuals, automaton-like, simply act out the roles scripted for them. Thus Hunter, on the formation of trainee English teachers within a Kleinian English pedagogy: 'this is the form in which the student *internalizes* the function of moral surveillance itself: finding in himself the onerous ethical antinomies and thereby beginning to shape a "balanced" self as the condition of shaping the selves of others.' Or, referring to an earlier form of progressive English teaching: 'Through adjustive techniques not unlike those which Donzelot has isolated in modern psychology, literary pedagogy *permits social norms to surface as personal desires* and personal desires to become the stake in social regulation.' Or Nikolas Rose on the family:

> The modern private family remains intensively governed, it is linked in so many ways with social, economic, and political objectives. But government here acts not through mechanisms of social control and subordination of the will, but through the *promotion* of subjectivities, the *construction* of pleasures and ambitions, and the *activation of* guilt, anxiety, envy, and disappointment. The new relational technologies of the family *are installed within us, establishing* a particular psychological way of viewing our family lives and speaking about them, *urging* a constant scrutiny of our inherently difficult interactions with our children and each other, a constant judgement of their consequences for health, adjustment, development, and the intellect. The tension generated by the gap between normality and actuality *bonds* our personal projects inseparably to expertise.

In this dance of language about what is going on in the transactions between the cybernetics and the organism – all this internalizing, surfacing, promoting, constructing, activating, installing, establishing, urging and bonding – is it ever made clear exactly *how* social norms inform the texture of experience or how they are transformed in the process?[3]

For Hunter and Rose, this is a non-issue. In an article on representation, Hunter dismisses 'formal' modes of textual analysis because their conception of 'subjectivity' is limiting and reductionist: 'Social agency has no general form (subjectivity) whose structure can be read off from a theoretical analysis of meaning of the "subject-positions" made available by a linguistic system.' Nikolas Rose invokes Marcel Mauss to make the argument that 'the self' is a contingent social category. Quite correctly, he starts from the premiss that, in the interplay between knowledge and power, historically variable definitions of the normal and the pathological act on, constrain and, in some sense, constitute populations and individuals:

'The self' does not pre-exist the forms of its social recognition; it is a heterogeneous and shifting resultant of the social expectations targeted upon it, the social duties accorded it, the norms according to which it is judged, the pleasures and pains that entice and coerce it, the forms of self-inspection inculcated in it, the languages according to which it is spoken about and about which it learns to account for itself in thought and speech.

From this, however, he seems to infer that when social norms surface as personal desires, they will not have gone through the radical process of negotiation and transformation that Foucault referred to as *folding*. In Rose's account, the panoptic gaze of the apparatus sees all. Nothing is invisible or unknown; the subject should be no problem.[4]

And yet, as Rose admits in the comments on the family quoted above, the subject is always the problem. Even when 'the new relational technologies of the family are installed within us' there is still a 'gap between normality and actuality'. This makes relationships within the family 'inherently difficult'. The machinery never quite works:

The modern family ... is a machine held together by the vectors of desire, and can only function through the desires that its members have for one another, and the operation of the family as a place where desires for the fulfilment of the self can be satisfied. Yet the incitement of 'social' desires required to fuel the familial mechanism is always threatened by the simultaneous incitement of desires out of bounds, anti-social desires, which can be satisfied only at the price of the destruction of that very socialization the family is to achieve.[5]

If there is no self preceding the operations of the social machinery, however, where do these transgressive desires come from? What is there to make the machinery malfunction? Or does the problem only present itself in this way because Rose quietly reimports a pre-formed self as the necessary target on which the machinery works – 'the new technologies of the family are installed *within us*'?

One way out of this difficulty is to take his '*gap* between normality and actuality' and rethink it as a splitting, a coding of different desires, conducts and destinies into the licit and the illicit, the normal and the marginal, the healthy and the pathological. This suggests that the production of the self does not work just through the incitement of desires. Rather, the norms *and prohibitions* instituted within social and cultural technologies are folded into the unconscious so that they 'surface' not just as 'personal desires' but in a complex and unpredictable dynamic of desire, guilt, anxiety and displacement. Subjects have desires that they do not want to have; they reject them at the cost of guilt and anxiety. Subjects are thus split from desires that remain incited but unrealized. It is only in the splitting that accompanies the interiorization of norms and the repression of incited-but-prohibited wishes and fantasies that consciousness and the ego are formed. This creation of the unconscious through repression is thus also the moment of individuation that allows conscious, intentional, autonomous agency within the terms of identification established through the authority of the social machinery.

In this revised model, the *repression* of desires is as important to the formation of subjectivity as their incitement: it is a mechanism determining the form of expression of the repressed material and prompting its repetition. Ian Hunter and Nikolas Rose present desire not only as an *effect* of the machinery of the social, but also as its *realization*. I am arguing that it is only through repression, the unconscious and the splitting of the subject – all the guilty secrets of love, conscience and fantasy – that the authority of institutions and disciplines can be secured, however precariously. From this perspective, which can also claim lineage from Mauss, individual psychical responses are translations of a collective symbolic system but are not in an isomorphic relation to it.[6]

The splitting – rather than the gap – 'between normality and actuality' thus sets in train a movement or a series of transactions. The unconscious that is necessary to make sense of the negotiation of authority as agency and the translations of the pedagogic into the performative is not a kernel of hidden authenticity, the real me, human nature. It is not intimate but, in Lacan's terms, extimate. In Lévi-Strauss's sense, the unconscious provides 'the common and specific character of social facts'.

The unconscious would thus be the mediating term between self and others. Going down into the givens of the unconscious, the extension of our understanding, if I may put it thus, is not a movement towards ourselves; we reach a level which seems strange to us, not because it harbours our most secret selves but (much more normally) because, without requiring us to move outside ourselves, it enables us to coincide with forms of activity which are both at once *ours* and *other.*

These forms of activity do not just 'surface' as individual desires and self-directed agency. Rather, they have to return transformed, as representations. They pass through a third space that is neither outside nor inside, but that psychic reality which Lacan located as '*the between perception and consciousness*'. This is the scene of negotiation, of enunciation, of that active fantasy life which supports reality by giving it the appearance of consistency.[7]

Fantasy in this sense does not imply an escape from the process of subjectification. Rather, it refers to one of the most important moments in that process: the staging and imaging of the subject and its desire in relation to complex social-symbolic scenarios. The concept thus allows an account of subjective investment in the apparatus and its systems of signification which does not prejudge the particular paths the subject's desire will take, or its shifting and multiple identifications in relation to the social and cultural field. It also suggests the costs of this fantasmatic investment. The security achieved through the consistency of the fantasy construction entails a narcissism that is necessarily in conflict with the demands of social relations. In negotiating the self-images provided by (for example) education and popular culture, the self never fully recognizes itself. It remains suspicious that there must be something more than the norms and banal transgressions on display. 'What one loves in one's image is something *more* than the image,' argues Joan Copjec. 'Thus is narcissism the source of the malevolence with which the subject regards its image, the aggressivity it unleashes on all its own representations. And thus does the subject come into being as a transgression of, rather than in conformity to, the law.'[8]

Here I have only skimmed the surface of a difficult and long-running debate. My limited aim has been to sketch the sort of theory of subjectivity necessary to sustain my broader account of the dynamics between the pedagogic and the performative in education and popular culture. The underlying moral is simple enough: that the dynamics of subjectification are more complicated and more painful than simply identifying with, or re-enacting, the attributes and behaviours prescribed by social and cultural technologies. The model I have suggested should, I hope, make it possible to begin to answer Jacqueline Rose's questions, which I introduced earlier, about 'how fantasy can operate as legitimation' and about 'the precise forms of identification and transmission at the heart of the institution'.

In the study of education, for example, this sort of approach has been developed by Valerie Walkerdine and her colleagues in exploring how girls negotiate the symbolic categories and connotations of mathematics in the school. They insist that the perceived 'failure' of girls in mathematics at secondary school cannot be explained either by psychological notions of development or by a more sociological emphasis on teacher expectations or pedagogic styles. The process involves a much more complex dynamic between the pedagogic and the performative. In the practices of the school and the family – and especially through the mother–daughter relationship – the authoritative categories of rationality and irrationality, masculinity and femininity, cleverness and stupidity, mastery and subservience, compliance and resistance are instituted in relation to each other. These are remixed by the girls as fantasmatic scenarios of desire, denial and transgression which return not only as a self-identification, but as agency. It is in the formation and exercise of the girls' mandated autonomy that, according to this evidence, the social and psychological injuries of sexual differentiation are systematically reproduced. This is not a formalist 'reading off' of a subject position from the institutional practices of the school or its disposition of discourses. Rather, the focus is on the sexually differentiated subject always-to-be-produced, always-to-be-enacted within its play of disciplines, technologies and symbolic systems.[9]

This perspective calls into question the image of the soul of the citizen being controlled or even regulated by the machinery of government. Instead, it reformulates the problem as the enactment of machinery and soul, of normality and actuality, and of authority and agency always in a dynamic relationship to each other. The unpredictable outcomes of this enunciation are attributed less to wilful rejection of government than to a more systemic resistance built into the circuits of subjectification. One aspect of this is the nature of representation: the way that it defines knowledge and information for a subject, and yet in ways that are inevitably partial and unreliable. In the next chapter, therefore, I examine the limits of representation, and the way that these affect the formation of social categories and actors. This focus reveals that the process is more difficult than can be admitted in, for example, the schemes to train active, responsible citizens, which I described in the previous chapter. There is always a dark obverse to it, a story of uncertainty, anxiety and fear. That is why I now explore some of the less respectable aspects of post-Enlightenment culture, as well as some of the more sublime.

Dracula. (US, Tod Browning, 1930.)

5

WHAT'S AT STAKE IN
VAMPIRE FILMS?

The Pedagogy of Monsters

Learn to go and see the 'worst' films; they are sometimes sublime.

Ado Kyrou

A typical American film, naive and silly, can – for all its silliness and
even by means of it – be instructive. A fatuous, self-conscious English
film can teach one nothing. I have often learnt a lesson from a silly
American film.

Ludwig Wittgenstein

'The story of the Devil, the vocabulary of popular swear-words, the
songs and habits of the nursery – all these are now gaining
significance for me,' Freud wrote in a letter in 1897. In 1914, he
observed in 'The Moses of Michelangelo' that the technique of
psychoanalysis is 'to divine secret and concealed things from
despised or unnoticed features, from the rubbish-heap, as it were, of
our observations'. This modernist sensitivity to the lessons of the
transitory, the elusive and the contingent is equally evident in the
study of the *Doppelgänger* published in 1914 by Freud's disciple and
colleague, Otto Rank. He took as his starting point a 'random and
banal' subject: 'a "romantic drama", which not long ago made the
rounds of our cinemas', Stellan Rye's film *The Student of Prague*.
Rank speculated that the nature of cinema may allow privileged
access to both 'certain psychological facts and relationships' and
also to 'the real meaning of an ancient theme which has become
either unintelligible or misunderstood in its course through tradition'.[1]

Although in looking at horror films and their pre-history I share the pedagogic impulse of Freud and Rank, my priorities are slightly different. I have outlined earlier how the networks of intersubjective cultural authority that constitute the nation-people are instituted through the routines and knowledges of education, literature and broadcasting. I have also stressed that these structures are always negotiated in the activities of learning, reading and listening. This dynamic ensures that official definitions of 'the people' must be unstable and anxious. That is why the dream factories do not manufacture only the latter-day rational recreations advocated by Reith and Grierson, or the compensations of a blandly delusory wish-fulfilment denounced by the Frankfurt School. They also disseminate instructive nightmares of violence, uncertainty and terror. In this chapter, I supplement my account of education and entertainment as governmental strategies with a history of popular fears.

One of the lessons of this history might simply be that the persistence of popular tales about vampires, doubles, golems and cyborgs lends weight to the idea that subjectivity is split and that identification is a mobile and unstable process. I try to take this familiar argument a step further, by drawing out some implications of Julia Kristeva's remark that 'the abject is edged with the sublime'.[2] Where the two overlap is in their concern with questions of liminality, and in their subversion of any fixed symbolic boundaries. This is the source of their terror, whether it take the form of repulsion or of awe. I therefore begin by exploring the literary and cinematic genre of the fantastic: its defining characteristics are the uncertainty of familiar boundaries and categories, and the delusions of perception. I then consider the sublime as a claim to cultural authority in Western thought from the Romantics to postmodernism. This opens up a new perspective on 'the popular' and 'community' that has political as well as cultural implications.

The Fantastic and the Uncanny

The usual way of trying to explain tales of horror and terror in literature and the cinema is to ask: What does the monster mean? In his essay 'Dialectic of Fear', for example, Franco Moretti invokes Marx and Freud to diagnose what is inscribed in the monstrous *metaphors* of Frankenstein and Dracula; he argues that it is specific economic, psychic and sexual fears. These metaphors also transform the fears. The relationship between capitalist and proletariat becomes that between Frankenstein and his creation. For Frankenstein's monster read 'a Ford worker', says Moretti; *this* is the fear of a dependent, exploited yet potentially – and dangerously – independent creation. As for Dracula, Moretti perceives in him the fear of, on the one hand, the blood-sucking financiers of monopoly capital and, on the other, the castrating mother. Perhaps to complexify the idea that in tales like this one thing can be read as straightforwardly standing for another, he suggests that these meanings are subordinated to the literal presence of the Count, to his metaphoric status. That is the point of transforming the original fears 'so that readers do not have to face up to what might really frighten them'. In 'An Introduction to the American Horror Film', Robin Wood uses a similar mode of argument. The basic formula of post-*Psycho* Hollywood horror films in the 1960s and 1970s, he argues, is 'normality is threatened by the Monster'. The figure of the Monster *dramatizes* 'all that our civilization *represses* or *oppresses*' – that means, for him, female sexuality, the proletariat, other cultures, ethnic groups, alternative ideologies, homosexuality and bisexuality, and children.[3]

My summaries inevitably sacrifice the sophistication and nuances of these analyses. Even so, both articles do flirt with a certain functionalism and a certain reductionism. For Moretti, the fear provoked by fictional horror is 'a fear one *needs*: the price one pays for coming contentedly to terms with a social body based on irrationality and menace'. For Wood, Hollywood horror is less compensatory than emancipatory. It unmasks the real Monster as the 'dominant ideology', that 'insidious all-pervasive force capable of concealment behind the most protean disguises'. The meaning of these fictions can be unscrambled confidently enough once you find the right code. History? Here's Marx with the answer. Repression? Wheel on Freud. Although they reach different conclusions about the significance of the monstrous, what Moretti and Wood share is an interpretation that depends on the *sociologizing of the Other*. This is also evident to some extent in this formulation by Fredric Jameson in his essay on 'Magical Narratives':

Evil . . . continues to characterize whatever is radically different from me, whatever by virtue of precisely that difference seems to constitute a real and urgent threat to my own existence. So from the earliest times, the stranger from another tribe, the 'barbarian' who speaks an incomprehensible language and follows 'outlandish' customs, but also the woman, whose biological difference stimulates fantasies of castration and devoration, or in our own time, the avenger of accumulated resentments from some oppressed class or race, or else that alien being, Jew or Communist, behind whose apparently human features a malignant and preternatural intelligence is thought to lurk: these are some of the archetypal figures of the Other, about whom the essential point to be made is not so much that he is feared because he is evil; rather he is evil *because* he is Other, alien, different, strange, unclean, and unfamiliar.

Certainly Jameson – like Moretti and Wood – is onto something important here. Images of the monstrous do help to define the boundaries of community, and tales of terror and horror no doubt provide some sort of 'defence' against the violence that is the root of the socio-symbolic bond. But does the recognition that such phenomena might be clues to overlooked or unsuspected aspects of cultural and subjective life neccessarily mean that they must also either reproduce or subvert capitalist–patriarchal–whatever social relations? The fit assumed to exist between the psychic, the historical and the 'mythic' seems too neat an explanation of such a messy area. By presenting the Other as a threat to identity, for example, Jameson ignores the *need* for an Other to define the terms and limits of identity. 'Whatever is radically different from me' essentializes both self and other. The image of an apparently coherent self repressing the irrational, the evil, the different disavows the fragmentation of subjectivity entailed by the very idea of repression and the unconscious.[4]

What seems to be missing from such accounts is any sense of eeriness, that disorientation of perception, which Tzvetan Todorov identifies as the key to the literary 'fantastic':

In a world which is indeed our world, the one we know, a world without devils, sylphides, or vampires, there occurs an event which cannot be explained by the laws of this same familiar world. The person who experiences the event must opt for one of two possible solutions: either he is the victim of an illusion of the senses, of a product of the imagination – and laws of the world then remain what they are; or else the event has indeed taken place, it is an integral part of reality – but then this reality is controlled by laws unknown to us.

For Todorov, the fantastic lasts as long as that hesitation. In contrast to realism's illusion of knowledge and coherence, works of the fantastic insist upon the delusory nature of perception – What's going on here? How can I be sure? Within this aura of uncertainty, Todorov identifies some of the fantastic themes of the self: 'the fragility of the limit between matter and mind'; the 'multiplication of the personality; collapse of the limit between subject and object; and lastly, the transformation of time and space.' The fantastic, in short, plays upon the *insecurity* of the boundaries between the 'I' and the 'not-I', between the real and the unreal.[5]

This seems obviously relevant to horror movies – the fracturing of the self in doubles and monsters like Dr Jekyll and Mr Hyde, Frankenstein, werewolves and the rest; the terror of its invasion by vampires, zombies or aliens. Yet Todorov's approach has not been widely taken up in relation to film. That may be in part because he was trying to define the fantastic as a *theoretical* rather than a historical genre: in practice it applies only to some Gothic novels of the late eighteenth and early nineteenth centuries and a few works that appeared in their wake, and was rendered largely redundant when the repressed and censored themes it was able to represent were incorporated into the scientific discourse of psychoanalysis. Another limitation on the usefulness of his theory in looking at cinema is that the fantastic requires the reader (or spectator) to operate in a mode of cognitive uncertainty. This applies perfectly to a film like Carl-Theodor Dreyer's *Vampyr* (1931). To the conventional interplay between point-of-view and 'impersonal' shots, this adds a third, disconcerting perspective, in which the camera seems to wander off in an arbitrary way and to act as an unidentified and unmotivated observer. Similar hesitations can occasionally be found in more popular films – Val Lewton and Jacques Tourneur's *Cat People* uses a variety of cinematic devices to keep the audience guessing whether the heroine really does turn into a savage cat or

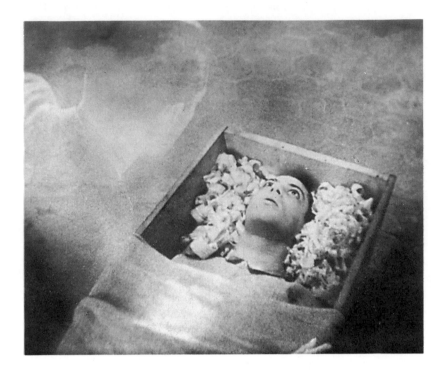

Vampyr. (Denmark, Carl-Theodor Dreyer, 1931.)

whether her behaviour can be explained psychologically as an effect of repressed sexuality – but as a rule popular horror films stick firmly within the conventions of cinematic verisimilitude. Also, although Todorov suggests that fantastic tales in the nineteenth century represented 'the bad conscience of this positivist [nine-teenth-century] era', his focus on formal characteristics and tech-niques does tend to leave many questions about 'history' and 'ideology' begging.[6]

   Is it possible to combine Todorov's stress on the textual mechan-isms of uncertainty, and on the 'fragility of limits' and the 'multipli-cation of the personality', with Moretti and Wood's more materialist concern with the historical specificity of monstrous figures? In an

The Cabinet of Dr Caligari. (Germany, Robert Wiene, 1919.)

article on social mobility and the fantastic in German silent cinema, Thomas Elsaesser argues that history is not a set of social and/or psychic fears to be metaphorized or dramatized in the films, but is enunciated in the narrative structure of the films. The inadequacy of any formal representation to this idea of history results not in easy homologies, but in excesses and imbalances. The vampires, golems, doubles, monsters and Faust-figures in *The Student of Prague, The Golem, The Cabinet of Dr Caligari* and *Nosferatu* should be seen as:

a displacement, an abstraction and reification of social and political moments. This displacement, however – being an unequal substitution, a 'failed' transformation – has left its own traces which manifest themselves in the intensity, the uncanniness with which the displaced and repressed elements irrupt into idyllic worlds and relationships.

Constance Penley makes a similar point in her study of James Cameron's *The Terminator* (1984), in which Arnold Schwarzenegger plays a cyborg sent from the future to assassinate the woman who will give birth to the leader of the guerrillas fighting the computers and their warrior machines that take over the world. This 'critical dystopia' of technology out of control, Penley argues, reveals 'a set of cultural and psychical conflicts, anxieties and fantasies that are all at work in this film in a particularly insistent way'. Although fantastic themes are evident – the fragile limit between matter and mind, and the transformation of time and space – she is more interested in the way a trans-individual fantasy scenario, the 'primal scene' fantasy of overhearing or observing parental intercourse, organizes a surface texture woven from the technological litter of everyday Americana.[7]

Penley demonstrates how this fantasy is worked into the 'time-loop' paradox, which structures the narrative of the film: if John Connor hadn't sent Rees back to protect Sarah, they would not have met and made love, he would not have been conceived, and so on. Such fantasies of origin are not, of course, restricted to the fantastic or horror. But these forms are perhaps particularly well adapted to staging them, not least because of the oscillation in identification that they demand. Their uneasy appeal is that what appears new and strange and frightening turns out to be something that, in a sense, we already know – we have a sense of 'moving towards a beginning', as Penley puts it. They are *uncanny* in the sense defined by Freud in his essay on the topic, published in 1919. They belong to 'that class of the frightening which leads back to what is known of old and long familiar'; that is, something 'old-established in the mind', but 'alienated from it only through the process of repression'.[8] We are dealing not with Jameson's 'whatever is radically different from me', but with something terrifyingly familiar.

Rather than trying to decode which repressed social and psychic anxieties are symbolized in the figure of the monster, then, the question becomes how the narrativization of fantasy produces the frisson of the uncanny. Nevertheless, Freud's essay does give some warrant to Moretti and Wood's attempts to tie down the meaning of the monstrous as well as to Todorov's emphasis on structural hesitation and Penley's insistence on the mobility of identification. Freud notes several times – particularly with reference to fairy tales – that the fictional representation of uncanny events is not in itself sufficient to produce the effect of the uncanny: 'that feeling cannot arise unless there is a conflict of judgement as to whether things which have been surmounted and are regarded as incredible [archaism and animism, for example] may not, after all, be possible; and this problem is eliminated from the outset by the postulates of the world of fairy tales.' This insistence on uncertainty as a requirement of the uncanny would allow *Vampyr*, but exclude *The Terminator*, which defies the laws of nature but leaves those of Hollywood naturalism discreetly in place. Nevertheless, critics have repeatedly shown how, in his own reading of Hoffmann's story 'The Sandman', which forms the backbone of the essay, Freud consistently represses most of its uncanny aspects in order to identify a single, coherent meaning and to justify this interpretation. Its narrative complexity, the intensity of its rhetoric and its repeated scenes of violence are all left out of account so that he can establish the 'scientific' truth of his thesis that its uncanniness is attributable to 'the *anxiety* belonging to the castration complex of childhood'.[9]

At the same time, observes Hélène Cixous, the partiality of this reading reveals Freud's own anxieties and repetition complusions; it is impossible to tie down the meaning of the uncanny as neatly as he wants to. What is at stake are the instability of the boundaries between human/automation or live/dead and the fragility of the limits of identity. The double should therefore be seen not as 'counterpart or reflection, but rather the doll that is neither dead nor alive':

It is the *between* that is tainted with strangeness. . . . What is intolerable is that the Ghost [or the Vampire or the visitor from the future] erases the limit which exists between two states, neither alive nor dead; passing through, the dead man returns in the manner of the Repressed. It is his coming back which makes the ghost what he is, just as it is the return of the Repressed that inscribes the repression.

In terms that recall the hero witnessing his corpse being confined in its coffin in *Vampyr*, or Dracula sleeping entombed in his native earth, Cixous conjures up 'the supremely disquieting idea: the phantasm of the man buried alive: his textual head, shoved back into the maternal body, a horrible pleasure'.

> Why is it that the maternal landscape, the *heimisch*, and the familiar become so disquieting? The answer is less buried than we might suspect. The obliteration of any separation, the realization of the desire which in itself obliterates a limit ...

It is in this 'confusion of life and death', suggests Cixous, that castration takes on its significance:

> It is the notch and also the other self of the man buried alive: a bit too much death in life; a bit too much life in death, at the merging intersection. There is no recourse to an inside/outside. You are there permanently. There is *no reversal* from one term to another. Hence, the horror: you could be dead while living, you can be in a dubious state.[10]

The Sublime

This sense of being in a dubious state connects the uncanny not only to Todorov's fantastic, but also to the idea of the sublime. The sublime too involves uncertainty and vertigo: *Can this be true? This defies imagination!* Some critics have therefore suggested that in 'The Uncanny' Freud stumbled upon a partial psychology of the sublime: *partial* because he attempts to exert his control over the sublime by reducing the uncanny to an infantile and/or archaic complex.[11]

What then distinguishes the sublime from the fantastic and the uncanny? The usual starting point for attempts to understand the sublime, at least in its post-Enlightenment forms, is Edmund Burke. He not only drew the crucial distinction between the beautiful and the sublime, he also insisted that the sublime is a theory of terror: 'terror is in all cases whatsoever, either more openly or latently the ruling principle of the sublime.'[12] It shares this with Todorov's fantastic and Freud's uncanny; it differs from them in identifying the *source* of terror. For Burke, this lies not in the perceptual uncertainties of the fantastic or the disquietingly ill-defined boundaries of the uncanny but in the sheer immensity of Nature – and metonymically of divinity. He invokes stormy oceans, wild cataracts, dark towers and demons to convey the forces that overwhelm human reason and imagination and produce a response of awe and terror: his sublime involves powerful emotions ultimately reducible to visceral processes of pleasure and pain.

At least two paths lead out from Burke's ideas. One, concerned primarily with the beautiful/sublime opposition as a key to questions of taste, leads first to Kant, who rejected Burke's physiologism and reformulated the sublime not in terms of the emotions it provokes, but in terms of the limits of representation and the need to test its adequacy to the Idea to be expressed. Whereas the beautiful consists in ordering and limiting representation – the illusion of closure through the framed picture or the complete narrative – the sublime points to limitlessness and infinitude. But what is most important for Kant is the possibility of conceptualizing the sublime in rational terms even if we cannot grasp it through our senses. We can conceptualize *infinity*, even though we cannot see it or even imagine it. Thus the sublime, even though it may be provoked by what threatens to overpower us, confirms our status as rational and moral beings in the positive moment of rational comprehension or moral confrontation. This is its pedagogic aspect. For Kant, what is sublime is not the vast or powerful object but the supersensible cast of mind which enables us to deal with it.[13]

Kant ruled out the products of human artifice as sources of the sublime, perhaps because art could entail the beautification of the sublime, and hence its containment. Already in Kant, the sublime was what resists the tendency to a closed, definitive system that is inherent in the idea of the beautiful. This argument was taken up by people like Schiller and Kleist, who saw the merely beautiful (and the sublime's true antithesis, kitsch) as collusive with the value-less world of bourgeois modernity in providing a mask of order and value for its real disorder. Hence the monstrous – along with terror, barbarity and tyranny – continues to appear in nineteenth-century art of the sublime as a tactic for transgressing the compensatory illusions of beauty, grace and reason.

There is a complex history as the idea runs from Kant through Schiller, Schelling and Hegel to Schopenhauer, for whom the sublime meant the Will contemplating itself, and finally to Nietzsche's distinction between the Apollonian and the Dionysian in art. Before following that through to Lyotard's formulation of a postmodern sublime, I want to trace my other history of the sublime. This runs not through Reason, Romance and Philosophy, but through a gaudier and more vulgar route.

The initial move here is to the Gothic novel (where, of course, we meet up again with the vampire). Like the sublime, the Gothic attempts to provoke awe and terror. Like the uncanny, its principal themes are death and the supernatural: this may be one way in which it provides a bridge between Burke and Freud. What the Gothic *adds* – especially through the absurdity and excess of its paraphernalia – is a new relationship to representation. By heightening the artificiality of its supernatural elements, it has been argued, the Gothic sublime of *The Castle of Otranto* foreshadows Freud's view that terror does not depend on a belief in the reality of what frightens us. Walpole goes beyond Burke by using these fictional elements, these representations, as a means of expressing and of evoking what cannot be represented – here, the materials of the unconscious.[14]

In his classic study of *The Romantic Agony*, Mario Praz plotted the high road from this anti-allegorical Gothic emphasis on the arbitrariness of signification as it was incorporated into the work of the Romantics, the Symbolists and the Decadent movement. That offers another route to a properly modernist, abstracting sublime. But again I take the low road, where the Romantic fascination with horror and perversity feeds upon, and re-animates, more popular traditions. The tale of how Mary Shelley's *Frankenstein* and Polidori's Byronic *Vampyre* were written is well enough known by now, but it is worth noting how quickly they were absorbed into popular theatre. The fact that by the mid-1820s it was possible to see a double bill of dramatic adaptations of *Frankenstein* and *The Vampire* at the English Opera House in London suggests the next milestone in this history of a vulgar sublime: *melodrama*.

Like Kant's sublime and the Gothic novel, melodrama can be

interpreted as a characteristically modern form of imagination. It is a symptom of the anxiety generated by a frightening new world in which the traditional patterns of moral authority have collapsed. The force of that anxiety is registered in the apparent triumph of villainy, and then dissipated in the eventual victory of virtue. To this extent, melodrama seems to perform the same optimistic function as kitsch. But it also shares with the sublime – and with certain forms of realism – the aspiration to get beyond surfaces. It attempts to reveal the underlying drama of what has been called 'the "moral occult", the domain of operative spiritual values which is both indicated within and masked by the surface of reality'. As in the Gothic novel, the unreality, the excess and the irrationality are functional: they enable us to conceive the unpresentable.[15]

In its more realist mode – in the serials of Eugène Sue or G.M.W. Reynolds, in many thrillers and 'women's pictures', even in *Dallas* and *Dynasty* – melodrama highlights the strangeness, the traces of this irrationality, in the familiar and the normal. This resonates with Schiller's view of the underlying irrationality of modern society, seen here not as a field of opportunities to be manipulated by the young heroes of the *Bildungsroman*, but as a cultural repressed. In its more monstrous forms – in Frankenstein, in tales of terror, in today's splatter movies – melodrama also figures the irruption of that terrifying irrationality into the everyday world. In making these links to contemporary popular forms, it is worth recalling Freud's comments on fairy tales, for the well-established moral categories and theatrical conventions of the melodrama and its successors increasingly work against the possibility of producing an uncanny or fantastic effect. In this world of virtue threatened by evil, the *mise-en-scène* usually ensures that we know exactly where we are. So where should we look for a modern sublime?

A Modern Sublime

Again, the distinction is between popular genres which display mysterious or shocking events within a naturalistic *mise-en-scène* – the Universal Frankensteins and Draculas of the 1930s, Hammer from the 1950s to the 1970s, splatter movies by Cronenberg, Craven and Hooper today – and a modernism which calls such conventions into question through its forms of enunciation. This raises the question whether there are *any* links to be drawn between, for example, horror films and a postmodern sublime – the neo-Nietzscheanism of Kristeva, Foucault or Lyotard – whose slogan is: 'represent the unpresentable'.

Although Kristeva's contrast between the semiotic and the symbolic might be read as a reformulation of the sublime/beautiful distinction, it is the ideas she develops about abjection in *Powers of Horror* that relate more directly to my discussion of Todorov and Cixous's accounts of horror and liminality. Abjection is that which does not 'respect borders, positions, rules', that which reveals the 'fragility of the law'; it is 'the place where meaning collapses'. Like Freud's uncanny, and unlike Jameson's notion of evil as 'whatever is radically different from me', it is an intimate and necessary threat:

> We may call it a border; abjection is above all ambiguity. Because, while releasing a hold, it does not radically cut off the subject from what threatens it – on the contrary, abjection acknowledges it to be in perpetual danger. But also because abjection itself is a composite of judgment and affect, of condemnation and yearning, of signs and drives.

The affinity between the abject and the sublime is that neither has a representable object, that both disturb identity, system and order:

> The 'sublime' object dissolves in the raptures of a bottomless memory.... Not at all short of but always with and through perception and words, the sublime is a *something added* that expands us, overstrains us, and causes us to be both *here*, as dejects, and *there*, as others and sparkling. A divergence, an impossible bounding.

Foucault's work on exclusion and transgression, dating mostly from the 1960s, also touched on aspects of the sublime. Like Kristeva, he uses a spatial model of Same and Other, in which the Other is inhabited by figures of madness, sexuality, death and the diabolical. This space lies between discourse and the unconscious, and these figures become visible in the form of a non-discursive language which transgresses its limit and invades the space of discourse and rationality. Although they may seem familiar from the Gothic novel, melodrama and the horror film, it is the form of enunciation that is important here. In non-discursive writing, language takes on an opacity, an 'ontological weight', which subverts the transparency of discursive language. It is within the *pli* or fold created by non-discursive language that the postmodern sublime is constituted.[16]

Foucault and Kristeva are less likely to invoke folk devils like Frankenstein and Dracula, zombies and master criminals, pod people and blade runners, than the modernist pantheon of Nietzsche, Dostoyevsky, Artaud, Blanchot, Bataille, Céline and Klossowski. Although the popular tradition of horror and terror gestures towards the abject, the transgressive, the sublime, or whatever it is, its representation as morality tale or melodrama places it squarely on the side of a moralistic mass culture, of petty-bourgeois kitsch. In an article from the mid-1970s, Kristeva admitted its appeal – 'from the most "sophisticated" to the most "vulgar", we cannot resist vampires or the massacres of the western'. Moreover, in such films 'the sillier the better' because the gunplay of a routine western or 'the alternation between horror and prettifi-cation found in porno films' may bear, both referentially and formally, relatively unmediated traces of the drive – the aggression – which motivates them. But the terrifying aspect of this terror/seduction node is soon domesticated in popular cinema; only the regulatory catharsis remains – 'in mediocre pot-boilers ... in order to remain within the range of petty-bourgeois taste, film plays up to narcissistic identification, and the viewer is satisfied with "three-buck" seduction'. Once again, with a saving clause for the authentically vulgar and silly, Kristeva displays the contempt and condescension for kitsch, which has always been the mark of the modernist sublime.[17]

Nowhere is this more explicit than in Lyotard.[18] His aesthetic of the sublime is a response to his vision of the radical incommensura-bility and heterogeneity of our 'world' – the ungraspability to which artists should bear witness. The mimetic conventions of realist art and literature are not just inadequate to this. In so far as they embody a constraining consensus of taste, they are part of the problem. It is to challenge this consensus and these conventions that paintings should always pose anew the question, 'What is painting?'

But what is the unpresentable that this avant-garde art of the sublime is supposed to represent?

This becomes clearer in Lyotard's distinction between two types of modernist sublime. In the sublime of *nostalgia*, the unpresentable is an absent *content* – a lost presence experienced by the human subject – which is presented in reassuringly familiar *form*. Lyotard gives the literary example of Proust, along with artists like Fuseli, Friedrich, Delacroix, Malevich, the German Expressionists and de Chirico. (So if my 'popular' sublime could sneak in anywhere, it would be here.) *Novatio* – the genuine sublime sentiment – presents the unpresentable in the form itself, emphasizing 'the increase of being and the jubilation which result from the invention of new rules of the game, be it pictorial, artistic, or any other'. Thus, *contra* Proust, Joyce; and in the visual arts, Cézanne, Picasso and Braque, Lissitsky, Mondrian and Duchamp. Such works of novatio are postmodern not because they fit into some art-historical periodization, but because they refuse art's institutional tendency to domesticate the sublime.

Why all this postmodernist fuss about the sublime? Doesn't it just elevate modernism's itch for newness to an aesthetic principle? For Lyotard, clearly not – as his displacement of the force of the sublime/beautiful opposition onto novatio and nostalgia hints. For him, the beautiful lingers on only as a term of abuse with which to berate Habermas and his dreams of art as a culturally healing force. The implication is that Lyotard's sublime always has a political as well as an aesthetic dimension. This is evident in the tantalizing call at the end of *The Postmodern Condition* for 'a politics that would respect both the desire for justice and the desire for the unknown'.[19] Here the 'desire for the unknown' is the political sublime that contrasts with Habermas's utopian desire to legislate the good society.

Can Lyotard escape the hold of norms so easily? Doesn't his 'desire for justice' itself imply acceptance of rules, of laws and of order? He claims not, because he inhabits a political landscape of discourse-genres cut off from each other by abysses. In this context, any claims to consensus or to identity – like the aesthetics of beauty or the politics of utopianism – constitute not just an unwarranted totalization, but a form of totalitarianism. And yet, Lyotard acknowledges, despite the absence of universal norms or agreed criteria of judgement, one has to act politically, to make critical choices. It is in this disenchanted desire for justice that Lyotard's aesthetic argument takes on its political force. The sublime suggests a way of bridging the gap between the aesthetic and the historical-political: if the sublime resides less in the artwork than in specula-tion on it, then it can become a model for political judgement. If aesthetic thought is characterized by the need to judge in the absence of determinable laws, and if Lyotard is right that there are no determinable laws in ethics and politics either, then the question of the *authority* for calculation within these spheres itself becomes the nub of the problem.

The sublime thus comes to indicate a tension between the joy of having a feeling of the totality and the inseparable sorrow of not being able to present an object equal to the Idea of that totality. The terms in which Lyotard addresses this problem derive from Kant's treatment of community. As David Carroll suggests, this is how the sublime suggests a new, thoroughly agonistic conception of political pluralism:

> Central to the feeling of the sublime is the limitlessness of its determina-tion, its aesthetic and political formlessness; in it there is a *demand* for universality, for community, and not the projection of a particular form of community as if it were universal.... The advantage of Kant's indirect presentation of the Idea of community for Lyotard is that the demand for community is felt even more strongly and can be considered universal (and thus just) only because it remains a *demand* and is not motivated or determined by any knowledge or intuition of *the form* such a community should take. The demand is there and is constant without, however, any rules determining it; the demand reveals the limitation of all rules, the necessity to go beyond them. In this way, the differences of opinion, the conflicts and disputes over the form community should take could themselves be taken as signs of the demand for community and not necessarily a threat to it. The real threat to community is when a state, society, class, party, or group pretends to know what true community is and acts to impose this ideal on society.[20]

For Lyotard, this projection of community constitutes terror. And that brings me, circuitously, back to the popular.

The Popular

Not that Lyotard has much to say about the sort of popular culture I have been talking about. He is as unremittingly hostile, or un-comprehending, towards it as Adorno at his grumpiest. More interesting is the way he worked through the tension he identifies between the *demand* for universality and the *imposition* of identity in relation to the idea of 'the popular'. In *Au Juste*, for example, he uses the popular tradition of narration among the Amazonian Cashin-ahua as an example of the pragmatic basis for ethics which he sees as an alternative to the classic Western explanation in terms of law and autonomy. The Cashinahua narrator is not autonomous in that he must first be a narratee; he has to hear his story before he can tell it. He is thus authorized before he is an author. He becomes a relay in the tradition, only identifying himself at the end of the narration: 'when he gives his proper name, the teller designates himself as someone who has been narrated by the social body.' For Lyotard this is a *popular* tradition in so far as the narrative does not become codified, but constantly has to be reinvented as it is repeated. It imposes an obligation to narrate, but this is not the same as the imposition of a particular content or a cultural identity:

> The relevant feature is not faithfulness: it is not because one has preserved the story well that one is a good narrator, at least as far as profane narratives are concerned. On the contrary, it is because one 'hams' it up, because one invents, because one inserts novel episodes that stand out as motifs against the narrative plot line, which, for its part, remains stable, that one is successful. When we say tradition, we think identity without difference, whereas there actually is very much difference: the narratives get repeated but are never identical.

More recently, Lyotard has taken a greater critical distance from this example of traditional, myth-based narratives because the derivation of the narrator's authority from the tradition eventually entails submission to an archaic 'we'. This leads him to deploy the same instance to make an almost contrary case. Rather than illustrating the demand of community through the obligation to narrate, it now suggests to him the problem of what happens when a 'politics of myth' is imposed in modernity, claiming legitimacy from a mythic national tradition and distant origin. 'We respect the Amazon peoples to the extent they are not modern,' he has said in an interview, 'but when modern men make themselves into Amazons, it is monstrous.'[21]

Lyotard's example of this monstrous politics of myth is Nazi Germany, but others can be found closer to home. The imposition of an identity in the name of an origin that defines the form of community – *the people* in the sense of *Volk* – was also a distinctive feature of the populist conservatism dominant in Britain and the United States in the 1970s and 1980s. Its adversarial rhetoric asserted the limits of identity by conjuring up the threat of monstrous or unnatural forces. 'The decline of contemporary thought has been hastened by *the misty phantom* of Socialism,' Margaret Thatcher asserted in 1976. Two years later came one of her most notorious utterances: 'The British character has done so much for democracy, for law, and done so much throughout the world that if there is any *fear that it might be swamped*, people are going to react.' After the miners' strike of 1984/5, they and their supporters became *the enemy within*. In such instances, suggests Jacqueline Rose, Thatcher was repeating 'one of the fundamental psychic tropes of fascism, which acts out this structure of aggressivity, giving name and place to the invisible adversary which is an inherent part of it.' Other commentators have picked up on this theme too. In 1984, after the Brighton bombing, Sarah Benton commented in the *New Statesman* on the dark side of the mystical Tory faith in national community: 'Such a belief can only derive coherence from the conjuring up of the Alien, a force whose shape you never quite see but which lurks in every unlit space ready to destroy you; and is incubated, unnoticed, in the healthy body politic.' For Laura Mulvey, the official narration of the miners' strike was more ambivalent, but still monstrous: 'Like the Frankenstein monster, the miners struggled for control of their own story, and like the monster, were cast simultaneously as evil and tragic.' And Michael Rogin set Ronald Reagan's view of the world in the context of a history of 'demonology' and 'countersubversion' in American politics:

The demonologist splits the world in two, attributing magical, pervasive power to a conspiratorial centre of evil. Fearing chaos and secret penetration, the countersubversive interprets local initiatives as signs of alien power. Discrete individuals and groups become, in the counter-subversive imagination, members of a single political body directed by its head. The countersubversive needs monsters to give shape to his anxieties and to permit him to indulge his forbidden desires.[22]

In his reflections on the social imaginary of Nazism, Saul Friedländer suggests how such terroristic kitsch, when taken to extremes, can promise total freedom through absolute submission to the authoritative identity.

On the side of the affirmation of order, the kitsch vision reinforces the aesthetic criteria of a submissive mass, serene in its quest for harmony, always partial to sentimentality.... But facing the kitsch aesthetic is the unfathomable world of myths; facing the visions of harmony, the lights of the apocalypse; facing the young girls crowned with flowers and the snow-capped peaks of the Bavarian Alps, the call to the dead of the Feldherrnhalle, the ecstasy of the Götterdämmerung, the visions of the end of the world.

In this strategic perversion of the sublime, 'the people' are kept acquiescent through fear. It is possible to read the equation between the sublime and the popular quite differently, however, as that which resists this sort of closure and submission. Here *the popular* connotes not identity but the heterogeneity in any social formation which remains intractable to such normative demands. This is Bakhtin's carnival or de Certeau's inventive tactics of consumption. Lyotard himself comes close to such images when he characterizes his Idea of 'the people' as 'the name of heterogeneous phrases that contradict each other and are held together by their contrariety itself.'[23]

This ambiguity between normativity and heterogeneity can be seen not only in the political deployment of 'the popular', but also in aesthetic or cultural arguments. Its mobility is something else 'the popular' shares with 'the sublime'. In a Lyotardian gesture, we might regard both terms as naming possible moves within the language games of politics and aesthetics. Their juxtaposition then becomes a kind of knight's move, an advance that sidesteps the given categories of either game and shifts between the two, using the rules of one game as a principle of judgement and calculation in the other.

In aesthetics, approaching the sublime through the popular immediately undermines the Kantian differentiation of spheres by highlighting the institutions of cultural production, the sociological aspects of taste communities and the political clout of cultural capital. It also casts a new light on Lyotard's investment in the modernist sublime. Judged from the perspective of, say, Pierre Bourdieu's sociology of taste, isn't this aesthetic as authoritarian as any other?[24]

Try that the other way round. How would a popular aesthetic appear from the perspective of the Lyotardian sublime? At first sight, no doubt, it looks like its polar opposite: a demand for kitsch, for the domestication of aesthetic experience as an adjunct of everyday life. Whereas the sublime attempt to grasp the ungraspable requires experimentation and distance, the popular demands the familiar and the delimited even when, as in melodrama and horror, it is dealing with anxiety, irrationality and death. But the popular always denotes a centrifugal force as well as, and in tension with, its centripetal pull towards consensus. That is why some popular forms – especially the more offensive ones – *share* with the sublime a transgression of aesthetic boundaries and decorum. So isn't it possible to argue, with the surrealists, that bad taste should take its place alongside the fantastic, the uncanny and the sublime in a carnival of resistance to the hegemony of the beautiful?

This could be one version of what is at stake in vampire films. They are not just ideological mechanisms for domesticating or subverting terror and repression in popular culture, as critics like Moretti and Wood sometimes suggest. They cannot be measured against a scale of political effects. They are better understood as symptomatic rather than functional: not as causes but as signs of the instability of culture, the impossibility of its closure or perfection. The dialectic of repulsion and fascination in the monstrous reveals how the apparent certainties of representation are always undermined by the insistent operations of desire and terror. The lurid obsession with archaism and liminality in horror films, and their play on the uncanny ambivalences of *heimlich* and *unheimlich*, high-light the fragility of any identity that is wrought from abjection.

From here, another move may suggest what is at stake politically in rethinking the popular through the sublime. Although Gramsci had in mind fascism's 'crisis of authority' in the 1930s when he remarked that it 'consists precisely in the fact that the old is dying and the new cannot be born; in this interregnum a great variety of morbid symptoms appear', he could have been describing those murky aspects of popular culture I have been looking at here. Gramsci's conception of crisis also recalls Lyotard's sublime in so far as both point to the way that established political categories and identities periodically fall apart: 'the great masses have become detached from their traditional ideologies, and no longer believe what they used to believe previously.' It is this dissolution of boundaries and identities that produces the 'morbid symptoms'.[25]

Lyotard's 'sublime' and Gramsci's 'crisis' undermine the status of 'identity' by showing that all claims to speak in the name of 'the people' or 'the individual' or 'the class' are assertions and justifi-cations of a particular mode of authority. In claiming to represent the known political *form* of community – its identity – they pre-empt the agonistic negotiations that should sustain the aspiration to communality. From this point of view, new, improved 'identities' provide no real alternative to the radical imperatives of a normative political culture. So could a popular politics perhaps learn from Lyotard to find new forms of calculation and mobilization modelled on the particularizing forms of aesthetic judgement: a politics concerned less with the people as an archaic myth of origins than with a pragmatics of the popular as an endless, disorderly dialogue?

Any proposal that mixes politics and aesthetics should set off alarm bells. To aestheticize politics without at the same time politicizing aesthetics and so revaluing both terms is, as Walter Benjamin taught us, a move to fascism. The step I am trying to imagine leads in a different direction. It indicates a cultural politics and a political culture that would take heterogeneity and frag-mentation, those blunt and comic facts of life, seriously. In this alternative, will-o'-the-wisp 'identities' would still be conjured up by the dynamics of fantasy and desire, by the operation of cultural technologies, governmental disciplines and systems of representation, and by the interaction between them – just as they always have been. But it would resist the temptation to found a politics on the expression or perfection of such identities. Instead, as Frantz Fanon insisted in a phrase that recalls the uncertainties and hesitations of Todorov's fantastic, 'it is to the zone of occult instability where the people dwell that we must come'.[26] What would a politics appropriate to such a shadowy borderland look like? It would still require worldly political calculation – always that. From the sublime it might learn an attention to the materiality and limits of representation, and to their inevitable inadequacy to the idea of totality; and from this acknowledgment of the impossibility of government, it might also learn a certain pragmatic modesty. What could it learn from the transgressive and creative aspects of popular culture? One lesson, certainly, would be the impossibility of political closure, the dangers as well as the mobilizing force of identities and utopias. Another lesson would therefore be the need to take account of popular fears and anxieties, but without exploiting them or pandering to them. This politics would be aware of the possibilities implicit in the critical manipulation and enjoyment of symbolic forms, the pleasures of the confusion of boundaries, and so also sensitive to the need for responsibility in the aspiration towards community that always remains to be brought into being.[27] Maybe, taking our cue from what Wittgenstein learnt in his afternoons at the cinema, this could be a line of thought opened up by a despised and silly popular form like the vampire film.

6

MRS THATCHER'S LEGACY

The Re-regulation of Broadcasting and Education

... the boundary between science fiction and social reality is an optical illusion.

Donna Haraway

... a politics that would respect both the desire for justice and the desire for the unknown.

Jean-François Lyotard

In the early monetarist days of her first government, Margaret Thatcher spelt out the evangelical ambition of her political programme. 'Economics is the method,' she said. 'The aim is to change the soul.' From 1979 until the coup that toppled her in 1990, the terroristic kitsch of 'Thatcherism' was fuelled by a sentimental, dreadful faith in 'the nation', 'the family' and 'the individual'. In focus, style and tactics, of course, there were many shifts and adaptations. But however pragmatic Mrs Thatcher's statecraft, the long-term agenda for social and cultural transformation remained in place. In the third term of her regime, from 1987 to 1990, broadcasting and education became priority items. Both became the object of substantial legislation aimed at changing the structures of authority they embody and disseminate. Although, at the beginning of the 1990s, the final outcome of these changes remains unpredictable, their effects will not easily be reversed, even given a different government. Against this shifting backdrop, in this and the next chapter I offer a fairly journalistic sketch of how these institutions have been changed. I also suggest how, if reformed and reconceptualized in very different ways, they might yet contribute to the creation of a more radical democracy.

In my account of the age of Reith and Leavis, I argued that it makes more sense to examine education and broadcasting as overlapping cultural apparatuses or technologies than to play the academic Savonarola and denounce the evils of the dream factories. It is not just that both school and television provide us with knowledge, values, opinions and images of ourselves and others. 'We' only come to exist as public and as nation-people as they address us in those terms. Their routines and rituals and pastimes shape the calendar of our years and the schedule of our days. It is through these intimate rhythms of community and normality, and these enigmatic processes of identification and differentiation that our liberty is regulated. This is what is involved in the radical changes now envisaged. Any critical alternative that is going to be politically effective, therefore, needs to understand and contest them as they attempt to redraw the boundaries of everyday life and to restage the categories and relations of 'the social'.

Changes

Both the Education Reform Act 1988 and the White Paper *Broadcasting in the '90s: Competition, Choice and Quality* (1988) reveal a familiar tension. Under the rubric of modernization, they combine a neo-liberal commitment to the free play of market forces with a neo-conservative espousal of cultural identity, authority and 'standards'.

The neo-liberal strand is evident in many of the major administrative changes proposed by the Education Reform Act. Among the most significant are the transfer of responsibility for financial management to individual schools; the promotion of competition by giving parents an absolute right to select their children's schools, which will be required to publish examination results as 'performance indicators'; the encouragement given to schools – or rather 'parents' – to 'opt out' of local education authority (LEA) control; and the increase of parental and employers' representation on governing bodies at the expense of political parties. In the broadcasting proposals, the impetus to deregulation lies behind the long-term plan to phase out the license fee for the BBC, probably in favour of some form of subscription; the abolition of the Independent Broadcasting Authority (IBA) in favour of 'lighter touch' regulation by a newly formed Independent Television Commission, which will include satellite and cable within its ambit; the promotion of 'consumer' choice; the awarding of the franchises for a regionally based Channel 3 and the new Channel 5 on the basis of a blind auction; and the opening-up of radio to a wider range of commercial and community stations.

The logic behind such reforms is that 'the market' guarantees consumer choice, and *thus* (there's the leap of faith) plurality and diversity. Free the individual consumer from the nannying of intermediate institutions, whether LEAs or IBA, and the invisible hand of the market will do the rest – that is, it will improve standards in education, and guarantee pluralism and quality in broadcasting. Although it is true that markets can be effective for the distribution of many types of goods and services, they are not necessarily the most appropriate or efficient mechanism for social goods like education and information. Nor are they natural or autonomous phenomena. They can be sustained only through the active political regulation of rules of competition. And once that principle of regulating markets is accepted – as it has been under Thatcherism, if not always to very great effect – then it follows, explicitly or implicitly, that principles of distributive justice become part of the calculation. It also becomes legitimate to ask whether the operation of markets produces outcomes which, although they may not be intended, are both predictable and undesirable, and, if it does, to adopt forms of regulation that would prevent or mitigate them.

In thinking about education and broadcasting, therefore, the question is whether the market is an appropriate mechanism of distribution and regulation. That will depend on two factors: first, the type of social goods (and/or social practices) that we are dealing with; and, second, the consequences that are likely to flow from their deregulation.

Does it make sense to think of education as a commodity or even a service? The legal requirement of school attendance would mean extending the logic of the market to incorporate a notion of enforced consumption: that is why 'the parent', not the student, figures rhetorically as 'the consumer'. Education is better conceptualized as a civic obligation or duty, and that requires a different calculus of interests and access. It also seems quite clear that the marginalization of local education authorities, initiatives like the City Technology Colleges and the Assisted Places Scheme, and the planned introduction of student loans will lead, if implemented, to greater inequalities in provision and access, with less equitable and more socially divisive patterns of achievement and qualification as a result.

Although the profit-oriented sector of broadcasting is more genuinely a market, here too the consumer and the viewer are only rhetorically synonymous. Buying and selling takes place not between broadcasters and audiences but between franchise holders and the advertisers to whom they sell air-time. Audiences have been less the consumers than the commodity. And although video and subscription might introduce more consumer-like mechanisms for signalling viewer preferences, the current trend is not towards a thousand independent stations and producers blooming in a free market. On the contrary, the market is increasingly dominated by transnational multi-media empires like those of Murdoch, Maxwell, Bertelsmann and Berlusconi. (The attempts at vertical national integration by Time, Paramount and Warner in the United States in 1989 were a defensive manoeuvre against this global cartelization; the shotgun merger in 1990 between the two British satellite providers, Murdoch's Sky and BSB, was another entirely predictable consequence of it.) Deregulation might create new investment opportunities for the few who can stand the entry costs. It would also increase the number of available channels. But whether it would enlarge choice for viewers in terms of diversity of programming is far more doubtful. It is equally questionable, despite much optimistic techno-babble in the early 1980s, whether the market in technological hardware will lead to more democratic outcomes. The gap between the information 'haves', with their interfacing computers, car-phones and satellite dishes, and the 'have-nots' getting by with perhaps a telephone and a portable telly, is actually increasing rather than decreasing.[1]

Whatever the rhetoric, then, and whatever the wishes of the wilder-eyed sections of the Conservative Party, education and broadcasting in the United Kingdom (and in many other countries) are not to be deregulated but regulated differently. This creation of a legal framework for the market is one side of 'modernization'. The other is the attempt to create a social ethos conducive to its operation – an 'Enterprise Culture'. This is what Mrs Thatcher meant by changing people's souls. The paradox is that the strategy of modernization has been articulated in terms of a social imaginary that is profoundly conservative. Mrs Thatcher's eugenist science fictions were written in the style of Samuel Smiles.

The logic of a backward-looking modernization is most striking in the proposal to introduce a centrally defined National Curriculum for English schools. For Kenneth Baker, the Secretary of State who piloted the Education Reform Bill through Parliament, this was supposed to provide an administrative mechanism for ensuring government control over what goes on in schools, not least through the national testing of all children at the ages of seven, eleven, fourteen and sixteen. The Secretary of State now appoints all the members of the National Curriculum Council. This Council determines the content of the curriculum and oversees its implementation, and is the only body that has to be consulted in this field. The neo-liberal critics who condemned such Bonapartism on the grounds that it interferes with the negotiations between suppliers and consumers failed to see that here it is not the operation of the market that is paramount, but creating the social conditions *for* the market.

Equally, though, the National Curriculum clearly signalled a desire to reassert the traditional norms of standard English, a narrative national history and a disciplinary vocationalism. I have already discussed Kenneth Baker's oleaginous 'Englishness' and my own agnosticism about the notion; as Gertrude Stein observed of her home town of Oakland, I suspect that 'there's no there there'. What seems to be indicated by the cultural claim or demand of this peremptory Englishness is, in part, an anxiety about the possibility of maintaining 'the nation' as a cohesive economic or ideological category in the face of globalizing pressures and the internal fragmentation of the national culture. Perhaps more significantly, it also reflects the resilience of the thinking already evident in Robert Lowe's view of education's role in maintaining social heirarchies within a more extensive democracy. There was more than a hint of his principle that working-class children should 'be educated that they may appreciate and defer to a higher cultivation when they meet it' in Kenneth Baker's utterances. This logic is taken to its conclusion by Roger Scruton: 'It is not possible to provide universal education,' he proclaims. 'Nor, indeed, is it desirable.' Education, as a privilege and a value, is useful and available only to a limited community of scholars. Others, not to be despised, require different civil institutions to prepare them for their humbler lot.[2]

From this perspective, the National Curriculum can be seen as an academic norm around which cultural differences were to be reorganized. Although presented as a means both of opening up opportunities (for some) and of reinstating a lost cultural authority, it is better seen as part of an educational strategy to compensate for the market's inability to produce the social conditions necessary for its own operation. Trapped within a Hobbesian view of competition, for example, many British firms have been notoriously reluctant to invest in training. Because this works against their own long-term interests, as well as the public good, state – or at least collective intervention becomes necessary to secure those conditions; here through the promotion of vocational education and training in both schools and firms.

The educational reforms of the 1980s cannot be explained solely by the logic of deregulation. They also entail a radically increased level of activity by the state to achieve cultural and economic goals. Similarly, the changes proposed in *Broadcasting in the '90s* represent a far from straightforward commitment to the free play of market forces. It is not difficult to detect in the White Paper a tension between the free-marketeers of the Department of Trade and Industry and the more regulatory thinking of the Home Office; it has even been read as a defence of public service broadcasting.[3] A significant degree of consensus remains about the basic purposes and structure of British broadcasting. Channel 4 is fulsomely praised, and the BBC with its two channels is to remain the 'cornerstone' of broadcasting, commanding roughly half the potential audience and so providing a non-profit-oriented source of competition. Subsequently, the government has – properly, if quite inadequately – introduced constraints on media ownership and quotas for television programming by independent producers to limit the market domination (and so, incidentally, the cultural and political power) of the major providers.

'Consumer protection' is to be ensured by the Broadcasting Standards Council, initially under the chairmanship of Lord Rees-Mogg. This was originally proposed, it is true, as a sop to the Mary Whitehouse 'moral majority' lobby, but even sniffing out sex and violence involves policing the market, as does its remit to guarantee standards of decency. If it takes over the responsibility for research previously undertaken by the IBA, it could become even more interventionist, and in potentially desirable ways. A more sinister constraint has been increasing government interference, both through the direct or indirect suppression of information and opinion, and through the manipulation of news. Here again *raison d'état* has consistently taken precedence over the free play of the market, let alone the freedom of information.

Overall, the political strategy implied by the Conservative restructuring of education and broadcasting for the 1990s seems to be less a 'rolling back' of the state than a redefinition of the terms in which social relations are imagined, instituted and contested in order to produce changes in the way that government/citizen relations are regulated. One way of expressing that is to say it is about changing people's souls. Another is to say that it is an attempt to redraw the political map. The new, utopian cartography would reveal a limited but strong central state, with the intermediate institutions of civil society being abolished, privatized, replaced or at least modified. In this light, the changes in education and broadcasting appear as a shift away from state-initiated social integration within a (broadly defined) social-democratic consensus. Instead, in a revival of a nineteenth-century 'contractual' model of social policy, the government would cease to provide social goods, even at arm's length, and limit itself to defining and defending individual rights *vis-à-vis* their provision. This is why the search for appropriate forms of regulation becomes so important. By playing down its role as provider in this way, government can present itself as *libertarian*, even though it may be acting in increasingly aggressive and even *authoritarian* ways in its supervision of the providing bodies.[4]

These accounts still only tell part of the story. In addition to the neo-liberal/neo-conservative axis, a second axis is needed to chart the political style of contemporary Conservatism. At one end of this is a totalizing pole: the mode of the *polis*, organized around principles of universality, law, citizenship, the nation and public life. At the other is an individuating pole, registering that 'pastoral power' which focuses on the microscopic monitoring and guidance of individual lives.[5] Both the distance between these poles and the attempt to integrate the two modes of power continue to be evident in the transformation of education and broadcasting – and much else in Britain at the turn of the decade, including changes in the law and the National Health Service. As in any attempt to describe Thatcherism – libertarian control, authoritarian populism, regressive modernization or whatever – only an oxymoron can do justice to its dynamics. The failure to appreciate this complexity and fluidity often left its critics looking leaden-footed, committed to versions of social democracy and national culture that have lost what radicalism they may have had in the days of Leavis, Reith and Grierson.

Responses

Much of the opposition to the Baker Bill, for example, sounded like a self-interested defence of the status quo by an educational establishment, although it was not only that. Too many critics glossed over the shortcomings of the existing system and so undermined the case for its undoubted successes. Often they continued to ignore the cultural aspects of education and the curriculum and so failed to articulate a coherent alternative vision of how schools might be changed for the better. At their least convincing, they merely reiterated the perfectibility of a flawed system.

Others with a greater sensitivity to the political and cultural dynamics of education took a more ambivalent position. Denis Lawton, for example, formerly Director of the University of London's Institute of Education and a longstanding advocate of a core curriculum, charitably described Mr Baker's National Curriculum as a 'missed opportunity' rather than 'a disaster'. Mr Baker's mistake, he suggested, was to opt for an 'obsolete, subject-based' curriculum rather than one that would reflect an *adequate* selection from 'the culture of our society'.[6]

Lawton's own alternative of a 'democratic, non-utopian reconstructionism' turned out to be a watered-down version of proposals first put forward by Raymond Williams in *The Long Revolution* (1961). There, presciently, Williams warned that the old forms of schooling and privilege might still give way to 'the free play of the market'. Against the assumption that the introduction of a common institution, the comprehensive school, would be sufficient to bring about a new egalitarianism, he called instead for 'a public education designed to express and create the values of an educated democracy and a common culture', and attempted to identify 'the essentials of a contemporary general education'. There was little immediate take-up of these ideas, not least because Williams failed to explain how, in the face of vested educational interests, they might be implemented either pedagogically or politically. Educationalists like Lawton and David Hargreaves increasingly turned back to them, however, when they belatedly tried to envisage the scope of a fully comprehensive curriculum. What emerged was the proposal for a 'core curriculum' – of which Mr Baker's National Curriculum was an uncanny Thatcherite recasting.[7]

Not surprisingly, Williams's conception was more humane and democratic than Mr Baker's could ever be. But there is a real question whether it could provide the basis for a convincing alternative. The problem is Williams's faith that, if only we could get the curriculum right, then schooling *could* bring about an educated democracy and a common culture – that, as Lawton put it in his response to the National Curriculum, it would offer 'a way of improving society, and at the same time developing individual members of society'. This emancipatory logic fails to get the measure of how education operates in the administration of populations and the subjectivization of individuals. Its ideal of a common culture also proves to be more common to some people than to others. It embodies a particular tradition and ideal of British radicalism: a very different notion from Mr Baker's Englishness, certainly, but still one held together by a normative community defined by its own boundaries of representation. Its claim to consensus inescapably also defines those who are excluded.

These alternatives thus remain within the same political logic of experience, identity and filiation as the Conservatism they reject. They do not imagine alternatives in the diverse patterns of cultural difference and oppositional affiliation that characterize the new social movements and other emergent political forces.[8]

The practical opposition to the Education Reform Act has taken a more mundane form, as teachers quit the profession, as working parties fail to deliver the desired 'line' on aspects of the reforms, as firms refuse to stump up the cash for the City Technology Colleges, and as the sheer under-resourcing of the enterprise threatens to sink it. Whether these forms of subversion and resistance are likely to benefit students remains, of course, open to question.

The defence of existing arrangements in broadcasting has sounded equally hollow, nostalgic and, yes, conservative. 'Close-down for the Golden Age' was the characteristic title of Melvyn Bragg's lament in the *Guardian*. The nub of the broadcasting establishment's defence is that *quality* and *diversity* will be sacrificed to American dross or Italian-style pornography. Thus the barrister and dramatist John Mortimer, for example:

> The structure which enables us to produce what is undoubtedly the world's best television service is not particularly logical or simple to explain.... Our first requirement is a properly funded BBC which maintains a standard of excellence against which the commercial channels have to compete. The next essential is to continue the system under which commercial franchises are given to companies prepared to produce good quality programmes, and removed from those that don't. Finally it is important that someone has the money and the incentive to produce expensive programmes, such as drama which costs around half a million pounds an hour.... If any crook or charlatan who puts in a huge bid can gain a franchise, that is the end of quality. This process [the franchise auction], said to be in the interest of wider choice, will ensure that a proliferation of channels will mean that the only choice available is the choice of a number of varieties of cheap rubbish.

The IBA's old method of allocating franchises had, in fact, combined a lack of any systematic or efficient planning with a startling lack of accountability; its attempts at public consultation were a farce.[9] Equally problematic as his defence of that system is

John Mortimer's studied vagueness about what constitutes 'quality'. Enough money for the sort of drama I write, the cynic might say; glossy mediocrity, say I. If one spelled out what the concept involves more prosaically – the range of programme types, the plurality of perspectives and opinions given air-time, the variety of audiences addressed, the level of investment in programme production – Mortimer might well agree. As he uses the category, however, it remains no more than an assertion of his own threadbare cultural authority. The criteria for judging what is valuable or desirable remain embedded, and so unavailable for public debate. This allows him to pull off another sleight of hand. In his uncritical affirmation that 'ours' is 'the world's best television', he conflates questions about the organization of production, about programme quality and about political regulation. As a result, the *concept* of 'public service' is equated with the existing (or pre-satellite) *institutional structure* of BBC and IBA. Even as the appearance of competition for the BBC is now presented as part of the growth to perfection of the best of all possible television systems, the parochial warnings of cultural apocalypse, which greeted it in the 1950s, are once more trotted out to denounce satellite and cable. So it is that the Golden Age critics allowed the Conservatives to present themselves as the radicals. *They* at least claim to trust the 'robust consumer', to make people responsible for their own decisions and to be breaking up the 'cosy duopoly' of the BBC and the ITV companies.

There is, of course, a more thoughtful case than John Mortimer's to be made for the public service principle. My point here is simply that too many critiques of the changes to education and broadcasting that invoke a common culture or the public sphere read uncomfortably like a defence of 'Keynesian welfare-statism' in the sphere of culture. Here as elsewhere, that is no longer a credible way of framing the question.[10] As a political strategy, it failed to deliver the goods either in engineering a significantly more egalitarian society or in managing the economy and the labour market efficiently or equitably. Its Fabian collectivism occluded more decentralized and participatory traditions of socialist organization. Its insistence that the state should not only satisfy but also *define* social needs all too often meant that provision is experienced as intrusive, managerial and bureaucratic. Its exclusive emphasis on a technical calculus of need, resource and provision also created a corporatist politics insensitive to the diversity of 'publics'.

Critics of Keynesian welfare-statism from both Right and Left would emphasize the monolithic nature of the BBC, its paternalism and its cultural arrogance. They would point out that post-1944 state education has often been 'unpopular' – that is, unresponsive and unaccountable.[11] They might also agree that education and broadcasting would benefit from greater *diversity* and *pluralism*, more *democratic accountability and control*, and improved *quality*. But that does not mean that the only alternative is to denounce everything that went before and to buy the Right's definitions of those desirable outcomes. Rather than defend the indefensible or slip despairingly into the arms of conservatism, it seems more sensible to return to first principles. So, like the nineteenth-century reformers or like the teachers, broadcasters and film-makers of the inter-war period, we might ask, what should be the purposes of education and broadcasting in a democracy? Are these purposes being achieved at present? And how might we judge whether the distribution and regulation of these social goods is just and reasonable?

Alternative Alternatives

Today the debate about democracy is largely preoccupied with finding more radical, extensive and diversified definitions of *rights, liberty, plurality* and *participation*.[12] The attempt to define reasonable limits to political power lies behind campaigns for a new constitutional settlement in the United Kingdom. This is needed, its supporters argue, primarily in order to guarantee rights that will protect citizens against a potentially – and increasingly – overweening state. However much Mrs Thatcher may have claimed to be rolling back the state, under her governments even these negative individual and civil liberties were eroded and many key intermediate institutions were undermined.

Such arguments often acknowledge the key Marxist criticism of the liberal conception of rights: the disparity between these *formal* rights and the *substantive* rights that people can enforce in practice.

The gap between the two is taken to be the measure of the oppressions and injuries of capitalism, of patriarchy, of racism and of other social divisions. This approach can lead to a lapsarian view of democracy: the idea that an ideal state of democracy did or could exist, but that the reality always falls short of it. But are these inequalities merely deviations from an ideal or an index of its corruption? What if one starts instead from the problem of how social relations are instituted in a field where such antagonisms are an inherent feature rather than an accidental one, and then asks how the social relations thus established act on individuals and groups? Then different, less idealist, conceptions of citizenship open up.

In their search for a more radical alternative to the liberal humanist view of citizenship as the individual ownership of rights, some writers have reconstructed the battle of ideas from which it emerged in order to reanimate silenced or forgotten perspectives: the tradition of civic humanism or republicanism to be found in the works of Machiavelli, Harrington and Milton, for example.[13] Here liberty appears less as an umbrella of rights to keep you dry when the political weather turns nasty, than as a capacity or potential which can be developed only by use. In contrast to the liberal premiss that human individuals making autonomous choices about desired ends are the irreducible constitutive subjects of social life, the organizing concept of this view is that human capacities can only be realized within appropriate forms of society. These require a community in which common discourses and practices deployed within common institutions 'identify' its members as citizens. Social relations are seen as constitutive of selfhood.

This suggests the special role of intellectuals and education in the notion of community, which Kant sketches in his essay on Enlightenment. There he imagines a universal educated public debating freely according to the disciplines of scholarship and civility, and in the process constituting the authority of Reason. This public could therefore act as a monitoring conscience for a republican government. A more sceptical account of the formation of publics would question any possibility of a universal emancipation from tutelage and also the assumptions about human nature that it entails: this is not how the 'governmentalities' of modern societies work. As

Foucault suggests, the exercise of freedom consists not in the enlightenment promised by universal Humanity, Reason or Society, but in unpicking the particularity and contingency of the discourses, knowledges and practices that define and form us as subjects.[14]

From this perspective, as I have tried to show, citizenship in modern democracies may be understood as a repertoire of attributes realized through disciplinary and pastoral technologies. Prisons, hospitals, the factory, the family, welfare provision, even sexuality (as well, of course, as schools and mass communication) embody the terms in which individuals experience and enact the social. These, rather than the authority of the legally defined rights, give substance to citizenship and the exercise of liberty. Rights and responsibilities cease to be metaphysical attributes of the person, and appear instead as socially conferred capacities and capabilities: governmental techniques produce the individual *as* citizen. Men and women participate in democracy, one might say, but they do not participate under circumstances chosen by themselves nor in the terms defined by the formal rights of citizenship.

The question is, then, how principles of freedom and equality are embodied in specific social practices, and with what outcomes. Because there will always be contradictory definitions of these principles, as well as conflicting interpretations of the outcomes and disputes over their equity, politics in this sense refers to the institutional *staging* of the negotiations between antagonistic interests, aspirations and identities. Civil society is the theatre for playing out this dialogue, and this is why apparatuses like broadcasting and education have become increasingly important in the exercise and mediation of power.

The critical defence of public service broadcasting as a prerequisite for a democratic public sphere – the analogue of civil society in the realm of information, ideas and communication – draws on a similar political logic. Writers taking this line seek to reformulate the concept of public service and to decouple it from the existing institutional form of public sector broadcasting. The principle they want to hang on to is that all citizens, however rich or poor and wherever they live, should have access to a wide range of broadcast entertainment, information and education. This programming should have high production values, and should aim to satisfy a diverse range of audience tastes and not only those tastes that show the largest profit.[15] The reformed institutions would be democratic to the extent that they are, on the one hand, independent from state control or market forces and, on the other, open to access and participation by their audiences. There would need to be constitutional guarantees of the free flow of information (against the secretiveness and dissimulation of the central state when necessary), the expression of diverse opinions, popular accountability and the tough regulation of corporate providers.

The BBC, however undemocratic its present organization and however vaunting its claims to universal representation, often remains pivotal in such arguments to the limited extent that it meets these criteria. Paddy Scannell insists that public service must entail 'the provision of *mixed* programmes on *national* channels'.[16] In many ways, this echoes Reith's vision of broadcasting's social function. This required, Reith knew, the 'brute force of monopoly' if he was to create and defend a *national* rather than a commercial broadcasting system in which the *mix* of programmes was determined by a normative vision of an integrated culture. That cultural monopoly no longer exists. Nor is the idea that cultural heterogeneity can be contained within a single, unifying discourse any longer acceptable, either intellectually or politically. The arguments in favour of a broadcasting system that *embodies* diversity rather than claiming to *represent* it therefore become more compelling. This suggests the extension of the original Channel 4 model of 'publishing' independently produced programmes as against the BBC model of 'speaking for the nation'. But isn't that compatible with the sort of arguments about deregulation and diversification presented in the Government's White Paper?

It would be only under two conditions. The first would be that the free play of market forces in fact produced diversity rather than a concentration of production. The second would be that promoting competition among independent production companies broadened broadcasting's *cultural* range and encouraged stylistic innovation. The evidence of most commercial television provision suggests these would not be met. The lobby for the introduction of Channel 4 in the late 1970s and early 1980s, for example, was a pragmatic alliance between two quite distinct 'independent' production sectors. One consisted of freelance producers and small production companies offering a traditional television product, but wanting to operate outside the structures and constraints of the BBC and the major commercial franchise holders. The other 'independents' were defined more in cultural, aesthetic or sometimes political terms: a coalition stretching from the radical heirs of Grierson to the experimental avant-garde. Although the Conservative government that set up the channel was probably more persuaded by the arguments of the former group for breaking up the near-monopolistic power of the existing producers, in its early days Channel 4 was genuinely more open than its rivals. Nevertheless, even then it managed to incorporate a diversity of 'voices', styles and traditions without allowing them to challenge the consensual principles and categories that constituted its frame of cultural authority.

To ask how potentially subversive voices might be articulated within a dialogue to be staged by broadcasting suggests where this line of argument differs from a post-Habermasian public sphere approach. In so far as that entails a utopian vision of communication free from domination, it remains within a lapsarian or Enlightenment conception of democracy. Although there can be no such end to political negotiation, however, any more than there can be an end to relations of power, that does not mean that things cannot be different – or better. Hence Lyotard's linkage between 'the desire for justice and the desire for the unknown'. Existing forms of legitimacy can be put in crisis by new perspectives that challenge their established norms of justice and reasonableness, even though it remains necessary to regulate the negotiations of the political according to such norms. According to Claude Lefort, this indeterminacy is at the very heart of the social logic of democracy:

> The legitimacy of power is based on the people; but the image of popular sovereignty is linked to the image of an empty place, impossible to occupy, such that those who exercise public authority can never claim to appropriate it. Democracy combines these two apparently contradictory principles: on the one hand, power emanates from the people; on the other, it is the power of nobody.

Lefort's conclusion that 'the quest for identity cannot be separated from the experience of division' is clearly at odds with the Reithian vision of broadcasting as the integrating force in a mass society which could address, and thus institute, a divided population as the One of the nation-people. It also explains my hesitation about Paddy Scannell's defence of the BBC on the grounds that it has produced a 'new kind of *general* public' and established 'new, interactive relationships between public and private life which have helped to normalize the former and to socialize the latter'. Whereas for him this democratization constitutes partial emancipation, to me it sounds like broadcasting's contribution to the definition and articulation of social relations and its ascription of dispositions and competences to the members of the 'public' it brings into being.[17]

The point at issue here – as it was in the system of national broadcasting established by the BBC between the wars – is how structures of cultural authority are instituted through broadcasting, and how these are negotiated in practice by their audiences. Now, of course, the political, economic and technological context has changed dramatically. There can be no return to Reith. Equally, though, there is little value in projects for utopian broadcasting systems which disavow the complexity and diffusion of power. What I have stressed instead are the contingency and the historicity not only of existing broadcasting institutions and of the proposed reforms, but of any conceivable transformations.

At the end of the previous chapter, I suggested three strands in a tactical, liminal politics that might tolerate this contingency. First, I defended the principle of worldly political calculation. In the case of broadcasting, major shifts are underway in the roles of the state and transnational corporations, and in the balance of forces between them. In the United Kingdom, although the status of the BBC and the public service ethic remain very powerful, the state's role as an arm's-length provider is diminishing. This will make the machinery through which it regulates both public and commercial providers all the more important. The debates about the levels and forms of funding, about the number and allocation of channels and stations, about the criteria for holding a franchise, and about the limits of what may be seen and heard all remain vital. Their outcomes will have a significant impact on both the economic and cultural prospects for broadcasting. They will also determine the texture of public life as they are translated into criteria of authority within broadcasting: who has the right to speak, who they are authorized to speak for, and in what form. At this level, the institutional arrogance of the BBC seems remarkably undiminished in its assumption that it can speak for all parts of a highly differentiated population. This is the flaw Rupert Murdoch latches on to so effectively in his populist case for the market. True, he offers only a freedom to consume, not the right to be heard: who gets to speak on Sky? But then, the idea of 'letting people speak for themselves' is no real answer – as the problems created by the Greater London Council's cultural policies in the early 1980s revealed.[18] It simply restates the familiar problems of authority and representation in a different register. The claim to represent or speak for a community is always a claim to know the identity and limits of that group, and so also a denial of its agonism and contingency.

Here the debates about the institutional staging of public life shade into the second political strand I identified: the productivity and limits of representation. The presumption to speak for a particular social group – representation in the sense of *Vertretung* – is undermined by Lefort's image of democratic authority as an empty place. And yet groups cannot become effective social actors except through the articulation of an identifiable voice; that is, through representation in the other sense of *Darstellung*. This is why the critique of the symbolic conventions of broadcasting is so important. The staging of current affairs and public debate, the narratological and generic conventions of television fiction, the invocation of specific audiences: all these play a vital part in defining and articulating forms of knowledge, social identities, and the relationships between them. Television produces a perpetual stream of new and familiar stories about both everyday life and the arcane worlds of art, politics or science, and in doing so establishes certain patterns of understanding as coherent, plausible and authoritative. Its cultural power is thus to embody 'the strategic narratives and rhetoric of a nation's public texts'.[19]

This cultural space of the nation is never wholly colonized, of course. It is not just where 'the people' are spoken, but also where people speak. This, then, is the third strand of a cultural politics: the creative activities of audiences in negotiating imposed practices and provided texts. These tactics of everyday life cannot be reduced to the notion of a reactive or epiphenomenal resistance. As de Certeau insists, they have their own logic and their own priorities:

> In reality a rationalized, expansionist, centralized, spectacular and clamorous production is confronted by an entirely different kind of production, called 'consumption' and characterized by its ruses, its fragmentation (the result of circumstances), its poaching, its clandestine nature, its tireless but quiet activity, in short by its quasi-invisibility, since it shows itself not in its own products, but in an art of using those imposed on it.[20]

Here de Certeau shows why popular culture is always the joker in debates about the public sphere, civil society and radical democracy. Communication can never be free from domination, nor can all parties be relied on to respect the rules governing social interchanges. The air is too thick with the babble of other stories, other voices and other musics, which reactivate the memory of old and recurring antagonisms. These should not be discounted as distortions or interference. Rather, this noise constitutes the range of cultural reference through which listeners creatively mis-hear. It is in this disjunctive creativity of popular culture that the dynamic between authority and agency is acted out.

This is not to devalue the concepts of public sphere, civil society and radical democracy. On the contrary, if read across the creativity and indeterminacy of popular culture, they make it possible to pose questions about the formation of community and tradition in ways quite different from either post-Thatcherite Conservatism or nostalgic welfare-statism. What they suggest as alternative perspectives on education is the subject of the next chapter.

7

DIAGRAMS OF CITIZENSHIP

On Education and Democracy

> But the work of education is constructive, not critical.
>
> John Dewey

> Socialism would take too many evenings.
>
> Oscar Wilde

In a lecture on 'The Idea of an Educated Public' – a concept intimately linked to that of a public sphere – the moral philosopher Alasdair MacIntyre describes teachers as 'the forlorn hope of Western modernity'. Why forlorn? Because they are charged with a mission that is both essential and impossible. Any rationale for education, argues MacIntyre, invariably boils down to the demand that young people be taught, first, to fit into some social role and function that requires recruits, and, second, to think for themselves. The particular nature of post-Enlightenment societies means that these imperatives of socialization and individuation are mutually incompatible. Only when critical discussion on shared terms is a *feature* of the roles for which students are socialized can the two go together, and this, according to MacIntyre, entails the existence of an educated public. His paradigm of such a public is the Scottish Enlightenment. This was by no means universal. Here there was a 'tolerably large' but self-consciously limited public sphere held together by mutually accepted standards of authority, canonical cultural references and shared modes of argumentation and justification. Informal debates about what constitutes the good life became institutionalized as 'both an extension of and an interchange with the discussions within its universities'. This was the consequence not simply of their curriculum or their agreement on issues of philosophical debate, but also of 'an understanding of their social roles by ministers, lawyers, merchants, schoolmasters and others, which enabled them in such local forums as town councils, presbyteries, boards of bank directors and law courts to look beyond immediate questions to issues of first principles.'[1] Without that sort of understanding and that sort, and scale, of social organization, an educated public is not possible and the two purposes of education – socialization and individuation – become irreconcilably divorced.

In tracing the emergence of this familiar opposition between domestication and emancipation, MacIntyre identifies the fault line that runs through much progressive educational thinking. This produces its disabling oscillation between utopianism and despair, as education repeatedly promises to liberate the creative human talents of all people and then fails to do so. Once it is recognized that, like broadcasting, education is an apparatus for instituting the social, not dismantling or escaping it in order to emancipate human nature, then what matters are clearly the principles that should guide its organization and conduct. In thinking how these might be negotiated democratically, the ideal of a universal educated public should not be set up as an achievable objective. If rethought along the lines of Foucault's agonism or Lyotard's neo-Kantian Idea of community, however, it might operate as an imaginative horizon, a regulating limit case.

This means going one step further than MacIntyre, and questioning his own opposition between socialization and individuation. As I suggested in my introductory discussion of Rousseau, the governmental strategies of post-Enlightenment liberal democracies work *through* the liberty and aspirations of individuals. Rather than silencing or constraining their desires and self-governing capacities, technologies of the self have attempted to attune them to political objectives. If individuation is the subtlest form of socialization however, so by the same token learning to 'think for yourself' is far from thinking *by* yourself. In practice, it refers to identification with particular symbolic rules and grammars, and thus socialization into particular intellectual and academic subcultures. It is not just that language and discursive genres necessarily pre-exist and constrain thought. There is also a paradox in teaching independence of mind.

If I as your teacher tell you to think for yourself, you are caught in an impossible position. Think for yourself, and you are still thinking as I tell you, in my terms. Think not as I tell you, and you must decide *not* to think for yourself. 'Thinking for yourself' is a state that is essentially a by-product, an indirect (though not undesired) consequence of some other social and intellectual activity: the learning of skills, techniques and information, participation in debate and decision-making, and so forth. What is at issue is less emancipation or liberation than styles of participation, styles in which subjection and autonomy inevitably coexist.[2]

This ambivalence, which is inherent in the exercise of liberty, is what makes government and education so difficult – especially democratic government and education. How might the ambivalence be regulated so that the different ways in which people experience it would be just and reasonable? This is the type of question that Michael Walzer has addressed in his attempt to formulate a theory of distributive justice compatible with a society both heterogeneous and egalitarian. In complex modern societies, asserts Walzer, the idea of 'simple equality' – everyone getting the same amount of the same thing in the same form – is neither achievable nor desirable. In principle, it is inadequate to their heterogeneity, to the real differences of power and aspiration that divide social groups. In practice, it could only be achieved by unacceptable constraints on individual liberty by the state. Instead, Walzer argues for a 'complex equality': the distribution of different social goods according to different criteria reflecting the specificity of these goods, their social significance, and the variety of their recipients. Rather than deriving normative principles that would apply in all cases from either the rights of individuals or the promise of universal emancipation, Walzer insists on a respect for the boundaries between social spheres and the negotiation of meanings and criteria appropriate to that particular sphere. In his discussion of education, for example, he suggests that complex criteria are needed to balance the requirements of a democratic polity with the different interests and capacities of individual students. 'Equal citizenship requires a common schooling,' he argues, 'but it does not require a uniform educational career.' So what institutional principles of association and differentiation, and what patterns of access to different forms

and traditions of knowledge, would be compatible with the requirements of complex equality, social justice and individual liberty?[3]

Amy Gutmann asserts as fundamental to her liberal case the
premiss that democratic education should provide 'the ability to
participate effectively in the democratic process'. Because this ability
needs to be universal, it has two negative corollaries which should
constrain the exercise of educational authority. One is the principle
of non-repression: unpopular (but rational) conceptions of the good
life and the good society must not be excluded. The other is the
principle of non-discrimination: 'no educable child may be
excluded from an education adequate to participating in the
political processes that structure choice among good lives.'[4]

A critical perspective on education can usefully learn from
Gutmann and Walzer not only their emphasis on the evaluative
criteria of *participation* and *accountability*, but also the principle that
justice involves a sensitivity and a responsibility to otherness. What
might this mean in terms of the relationship of democratic education to democratic citizenship? Translated into a British context, it
seems close to Raymond Williams's social democratic vision in *The
Long Revolution*. When Gutmann asserts that its priorities should be
teaching the *essential democratic values* and cultivating a *common culture*,
she is echoing (consciously or not) his argument that Britain's old
hierarchical and divisive forms of schooling should be replaced by 'a
public education designed to express and create the values of an
educated democracy and a common culture'.[5]

Bearing in mind the problems in Williams's formulation – the
dangers of assuming education can engineer the full expression of
either society or individual, and the limits and exclusions of the
community embraced by a common culture – what new possibilities and problems are opened up by this approach? How might the
emphasis on the construction of the social (authority) and the terms
of participation (agency) help us to think about the democratization
of education? I shall explore some of the possibilities and problems
by relating these questions to two aspects of education. First, I shall
unpick some of the rhetoric in the debate about access to higher
education. Then I look at the contemporary politics of literacy in
Britain and the United States.

What Do We Want from Higher Education?

Compared with all the ballyhoo about primary and secondary education in Britain in the 1980s, there was an almost eerie lack of debate about the purposes and provision of higher education. No ministers seemed willing to mount the classical conservative defence of universities as a bastion of the minority culture and the social elite necessary for healthy national life. The dominant tone remained utilitarian and populist. The main concern was 'for higher education to take increasing account of the economic requirements of the country.... Meeting the needs of the economy must be vigorously pursued.' Faced with this, many academics were unable to resist the temptation to sneer at the government's philistinism and to reassert, with little apparent irony or self-criticism, the virtues of their version of a liberal education. This was not just politically foolish, it was inimical to the creation of a more democratic system of higher education. Part of the problem was that the debate remained trapped within terms in which the concepts of a liberal education and vocationalism are inherently opposed to each other.

Perhaps the most famous expression of this binarism is to be found in Cardinal Newman's series of lectures on *The Idea of a University*, which he delivered in 1852 after leaving Oxford and converting to the Catholic Church. In the seventh lecture, 'Knowledge and Professional Skill', he addressed a topical question: what is the *use* of a university education? He did so by reviewing the arguments put forward in a controversy then raging between the defenders of Oxford 'liberal education' and its Utilitarian critics. The Utilitarians, he claimed,

> insist that Education should be confined to some particular and narrow end, and should issue in some definite work, which can be weighed and measured. They argue as if every thing, as well as every person, had its price; and that where there has been a great outlay, they have a right to expect a return in kind. This they call making Education and Instruction 'useful', and 'Utility' becomes their watchword. With a fundamental principle of this nature, they very naturally go on to ask, what there is to show for the expense of a University; what is the real worth in the market of the article called 'a Liberal Education', on the

supposition that it does not teach us definitely how to advance our manufactures, or to improve our lands, or to better our civil economy; or again, if it does not at once make this man a lawyer, that an engineer, and that a surgeon; or at least if it does not lead to discoveries in chemistry, astronomy, geology, magnetism, and science of every kind.

Against this, Newman's argument was that a liberal university education should be an end and not a means: 'a cultivated intellect, because it is a good in itself, brings with it a power and a grace to every work and occupation which it undertakes, and enables us to be more useful, and to a greater number.'

> If then a practical end must be assigned to a University course, I say it is that of training good members of society. Its art is the art of social life, and its end is fitness for the world. It neither confines its views to particular professions on the one hand, nor creates heroes or inspires genius on the other.... [A] University training is the great ordinary means to a great but ordinary end; it aims at raising the intellectual tone of society, at cultivating the public mind, at purifying the national taste, at supplying true principles to popular enthusiasm and fixed aims to popular aspiration, at giving enlargement and sobriety to the ideas of the age, at facilitating the exercise of political power, and refining the intercourse of private life.[6]

Three points stand out in Newman's argument.

First, he does not say that the University should have nothing to do with economic and professional life. He says that it can contribute to them *more effectively* through a liberal education producing certain modes of perception and conduct than through a specialist training: 'It prepares [a man] to fill any post with credit, and to master any subject with facility.' For many critics on both right and left, this is the root of the problem. British higher education, they argue, has continued to produce a *professional* rather than a *technical* elite. Bound together by shared values and a strong sense of corporate membership, and often hostile to the competitive values of capitalist enterprise, the existence of this elite has inhibited the creation of the social and cultural ethos necessary for industrial success. This interpretation of Britain's failings is most elegantly narrated in Martin Wiener's *English Culture and the Decline of the Industrial Spirit.* If it is not finally convincing, that is largely because Wiener too overestimates the capacity of educational institutions to form an elite 'world-view' that can be disseminated throughout society. His argument soon falls back into the binary view of higher education that I am trying to get out of: too much culture, not enough training. Just because a minimal vocationalism is neither plausible nor attractive, that does not mean that Newman's alternative of a liberal education would instil the skills necessary for effective management and a well-trained workforce. Neither position suggests persuasive terms in which to imagine what people could reasonably be expected to know and what they should be able to do by the time they leave higher education.[7]

Newman's second major argument looks back to the Enlightenment conception of an educated public and forward to Habermas's ideas about the public sphere. The University, he suggests, embodies and promotes the idea of a sphere in which equal participants can communicate free from domination. It thus creates the conditions for good and effective citizenship. As with MacIntyre's Scottish Enlightenment, though, his 'public' is sharply differentiated from 'the popular': Newman is talking about the 'true citizen *and gentleman*'. He is concerned with the ethos of a narrow class fraction, at times to the point of caricature – 'he knows when to be serious and when to trifle, and he has a sure tact which enables him to trifle with gracefulness and to be serious with effect ...'[8]

Thirdly, then, Newman's vision of the University has an ambiguous relationship to democracy. Through its autonomy from the state and the market it forms a vital part of an effective civil society. But this critical distance is sustained by the reproduction of an elite that perpetuates existing cultural hierarchies and a contempt for the vocational. Newman's University might perform a democratic *function*, but it would do so in an undemocratic *form*.

Almost a century later, in 1943, another cultural prophet proposed a not dissimilar vision of the University. In *Education and the University*, however, F.R. Leavis adopted a more pugnaciously oppositional stance against prevailing social norms than Newman:

[A]nyone to-day who proposes to take education seriously ... will inevitably find himself thinking of the problem as one of resisting the

bent of civilization in our time – of trying to move against the stream. . . .
The universities are recognized symbols of cultural tradition – of
cultural tradition still conceived as a directing force, representing a
wisdom older than modern civilization and having an authority that
should check and control the blind drive onward of material and
mechanical development, with its human consequences.

Leavis was as anti-Utilitarian as Newman, but he reckoned that the
rot had gone deeper, that the 'inhumanly complex machinery' of
modern life had led to 'social and cultural disintegration', to 'a
progressive debility of consciousness and of the powers of co-
ordination and control'. For him, the problem was how to control
this runaway machinery before it destroyed 'the human spirit'. This
would require some higher principle and mechanism of co-ordin-
ation. The University's role was therefore to bring 'the various
essential kinds of specialist knowledge and training into effective
relation with informed general intelligence, humane culture, social
conscience and political will'. The question is not whether to
produce *either* specialists *or* the 'educated man', but how to produce
both. Or, rather: 'The problem is to produce specialists who are in
touch with a humane centre, and to produce a centre for them to be
in touch with.' The University – and specifically an English school –
should provide that centre of cultural authority. 'Amid the material
pressures and dehumanizing complications of the modern world, [it
should be] a focus of humane consciousness, a centre where, faced
with the specializations and distractions in which human ends lose
themselves, intelligence, bringing to bear a mature sense of values,
should apply itself to the problems of civilization.'[9]

However seductive the vision of the University as the embodiment of critical independence signified by Newman's 'good citizens'
or Leavis's 'humane centre', Alasdair MacIntyre's argument shows
why it is impossible for universities to produce the sort of educated
public necessary for a participatory civil society. Nevertheless, his
lost ideal does raise the question of what role, if any, higher
education might play in creating and sustaining a more democratic
civil society and a better regulated and less inequitable labour
market. If it does have a role, if the whole thing is not just
Enlightenment nostalgia, how might this be decoupled from the

social exclusiveness of British higher education and its disdain towards vocationalism?

In the period of post-war reconstruction, there were several attempts to create forms of higher education more appropriate to an extended democracy. The new universities like Keele aimed, in Leavisite fashion, to reconcile expert technical knowledge with an understanding of culture, by which they meant 'the essential system of ideas governing the world and man, which belong to our time'.[10] Their curricula were therefore based on new and more inclusive 'maps of learning'. After the Robbins Report of 1963, the Polytechnics were supposed to extend the social reach of higher education, not least through a positive commitment to vocationalism.

It is true that the participation rate doubled from the 7 per cent of the eighteen-year-old age cohort in 1960–1, but, although this saw a marked increase in the percentage of women taking higher education, it did not represent a major re-allocation of resources to the children of working-class parents. It also seems to have pushed the system to the limit of what it can deal with in its present university-centred form, and participation remained stuck at about 14 or 15 per cent for a decade or so. At the same time, the relationship between higher education and the state began to seize up and the system entered its crisis of management and autonomy. This was the 'Robbins trap'.[11]

The underlying problem here is that access has been interpreted in quantitative rather than qualitative terms – more people getting more of much the same. Despite the post-war innovations, for most people higher education equals the three-year, full-time, post-school, single-subject honours first degree that became the norm at around the turn of the century. This pattern has been reinforced through funding, assessment, accreditation and entry requirements. Because the attitudes, values and institutional practices associated with 'the idea of the University' have continued to shape what people have wanted from higher education, the introduction of the binary system did not substantially change its academic nature. The parity of esteem the polytechnics were supposed to enjoy meant in effect judging them by the same academic criteria as the universities. Rather than offering more varied opportunities to a wider range of people, and setting up forms of technical and vocational education more responsive both to their demands and to the pressures of the labour market, the commitment to a demanding and largely uniform post-secondary education thus, inevitably perhaps, produced an 'academic drift' within the polytechnics.

Access to higher education remains partly a question of 'access for whom?' But ask also 'access to what?' and 'on whose terms?', and it immediately becomes clear that this is not just a question of numbers or simple egalitarianism. Rethinking the question in terms of democracy and distributive justice suggests not only that many more people should participate, but also the sort of qualitative changes that this would entail. What intellectual and vocational aspirations would a broader range of students have, for example? Some would no doubt still require rigorously academic courses, while others might want courses closer to retraining or to leisure. This diversity would require new criteria of assessment and evaluation. The *quality* and effectiveness of such provision would need to be distinguished from the narrower question of academic *excellence*. An audit of the whole system should not be derived from the performance of students taking one type of course.

The argument for extending access and diversifying the curriculum is primarily neither economic efficiency nor satisfying a market. Reform is necessary because higher education structures the terms on which workers participate in the labour market and citizens participate in the public sphere; that is, how they are able to exercise their liberty. Resistance to change is often expressed in terms of wanting nothing but the best for everyone. But when *the best* is imagined to be only *the academic*, that leaves most people with nothing. In effect, if not in intention, the argument is anti-democratic.

Literacy

'An illiterate person stands outside,' Lenin once remarked. 'He must first be taught the ABC. Without this, there can be no politics; without this, there are only rumours, gossip, tales, prejudices, but not politics.' This can be read as saying that literacy is a minimal requirement for participation in the political negotiations of civil society. Equally, it implies that mass literacy is a prerequisite for effective government by a state apparatus. 'Illiteracy is incompatible with the tasks of construction,' Lenin observed on another occasion.[12]

Literacy thus denotes both autonomous membership of an educated public, and yet also a technique of socialization. This ambivalence of literacy was evident in the different dispositions towards the standard language and the curriculum produced by popular education in the nineteenth century. It remains central to the cultural strategy of the National Curriculum. Rather than opting for a view of literacy as *either* empowering *or* oppressing, therefore, my argument is once again that literacy entails both the institution of structures of cultural authority, and their negotiation. This suggests a new set of questions. What sort of social good and/ or social practice is literacy? What problems is it supposed to solve, and how? What desirable outcomes is it supposed to achieve? At whom is it targeted? What knowledges are invoked in defining these problems, outcomes and targets? What are the ethics of different styles of teaching literacy?

With these questions in mind, I want to examine two symptomatic approaches to literacy today: E.D. Hirsch's *Cultural Literacy: What Every American Needs to Know* (1987) and the Centre for Language in Primary Education's *Primary Language Record: A Handbook for Teachers* (1989) (*PLR*). My choice of these two texts is not altogether arbitrary. In conventional educational terms one of them (Hirsch) has been perceived as traditionalist and the other (*PLR*) as progressive. My aim is to challenge the comforting stability of those categories, and to question how useful notions of emancipation or empowerment really are in assessing the purposes and outcomes of literacy.

E.D. Hirsch's polemic against progressivism has been widely represented in the United States as part of the same educational backlash as Allan Bloom's bilious jeremiad, *The Closing of the American Mind*.[13] It has had a remarkable impact there. Endorsed by conservative politicians and denounced with equal vigour by radical educators, it has spawned a generously funded Foundation running extensive research projects. Although not widely discussed in

Britain, its influence may well have filtered through into Kenneth Baker's initial conception of the National Curriculum as a catalogue of 'what every British child needs to know'. Nevertheless, to read Hirsch as just another sign of the New Right times is a mistake. His arguments represent, almost seventy years on, a throwback to the 'new humanism' of the Newbolt Report. Not only does he define problems in a similar way, he also invests the same desperate hope in literacy and literary education as paths to consensual citizenship.

Hirsch's approach to literacy has both technical and political aspects. His technical argument is that reading is a process of decoding words, phrases and clauses so as to recover the meaning a text contains, and that 'world knowledge' is a prerequisite for this process to be carried out successfully; if, that is, it is to go beyond a purely mechanical decoding. 'Although disadvantaged children often show an acceptable ability to decode and pronounce individual words, they are frequently unable to gain an integrated sense of the whole.' A full understanding is only possible when meanings are matched to broader cultural templates: 'the reader constantly connects a few words into clauses that have meaning and the clauses to appropriate schemata based on past experience'.[14]

This account of reading is linked to Hirsch's political concern to break the cultural and educational cycle which condemns disadvantaged children to remain poor and illiterate. His premiss is that 'all human communities are founded upon specific shared information', and that therefore 'only by piling up specific, communally shared information can children learn to participate in complex cooperative activities with other members of their community.' The problem is that schools 'teach a fragmented curriculum based on faulty educational theories' – specifically, Rousseau's 'content-neutral conception of educational development' and John Dewey's excessive 'faith in children's ability to learn general skills from a few typical experiences' and over-hasty rejection of '"the piling up of information"'. Instead, they should teach everyone, and *especially* disadvantaged children, the communally shared information that Hirsch catalogues in a List (his capital) of names, dates, events and concepts. In short, 'to be culturally literate is to possess the basic information needed to thrive in the modern world.' This need not mean mastering it in every detail, but having at least the passing acquaintance necessary to grasp the references and allusions in non-specialist texts.[15]

For Hirsch, cultural literacy is a social good because it allows the continuation and reproduction of society – which he interprets as a national sign community – and because it offers individuals the opportunity for mobility within it. In order 'to achieve not only greater economic prosperity but also greater social justice and more effective democracy', Hirsch argues in effect that the Enlightenment ideal of the educated public needs to become a universal reality:

> literate culture has become the common currency for social and economic exchange in our democracy, and the only available ticket to full citizenship. Getting one's membership card is not tied to class or race. Membership is automatic if one learns the background information and the linguistic conventions that are needed to read, write, and speak effectively. Although everyone is literate in some local, regional, or ethnic culture, the connection between mainstream culture and the national written language justifies calling mainstream culture *the* basic culture of the nation.

Here Hirsch shows that he is no conservative elitist and certainly no neo-liberal. He does not argue, as T.S. Eliot did, that the health of a culture depends not only on shared membership of a single national community but also on the differentiation of classes within that community. Eliot's premiss was that 'it is an essential condition of the preservation of the quality of the culture of the minority, that it should continue to be a minority culture'; his conclusion that 'a high average of general education is perhaps less necessary for a civil society than is a respect for learning.' Nor would he go along with G.H. Bantock's educational programme, based on this style of thought, in which the 'bottom fifty per cent of pupils' would be excluded from an irrelevantly academic culture and offered instead a 'popular education' consisting of Leavisite inoculation against the mass media, physical and emotional discipline and expression, and gender-specific vocationalism. In contrast to Eliot and Bantock, Hirsch is wholeheartedly a democrat. He wants social mobility, and he accepts that educational and cultural differentiation inhibit it by sustaining hierarchy and disadvantage. He wants *everyone* to be literate on the same terms, to have access to the power embodied in the national culture.[16]

Again in contrast to the conservative logic, he argues that the national culture is not simply the culture or language of one class, but to some extent an artificial construct which operates as a universal 'second culture'. Here Hirsch's argument breaks down. The national culture and the standard language do not need to be restricted in that way for literacy to work as a mechanism of exclusion. Their divisiveness works not through ownership, but through the different *dispositions* towards that shared set of signs and narratives. That is evident in Hirsch's subtitle. By defining 'what every American needs to know', he implies that those who do not know all this are in some sense *not* American. (The implicit racialization of his categories is especially clear at this point.) Although Hirsch might like to issue everyone with a 'membership card' of literate culture, the image of citizenship as a club only underlines the *limits* and *rules* of an educated public. Even if as a liberal-minded democrat Hirsch does not share Eliot's reactionary politics, he does share his vision and evaluation of what constitutes culture, and this pulls against his desire for democratization. Although he wants to expand the educated public to encompass the whole population, Hirsch actually shrinks the nation to the size of an educated public.

In that light, his argument can be seen to run something like this. First, he defines the problem as how to break the cycle of poverty and illiteracy. Next, he observes that the poor and oppressed do not generally read Shakespeare. Then he makes the startling claim that they are poor and oppressed *because* they don't read Shakespeare. Finally, from this unwarranted assumption he deduces that, if they can be taught to read Shakespeare, they will no longer be poor and oppressed. Of course, I am caricaturing. Hirsch does not only mean Shakespeare, nor even high culture as traditionally conceived. But whether the content of the List is right or wrong is largely beside the point. My objection is that the structure of his argument – the way he formulates the problem and its possible solutions – is itself fundamentally flawed. Although it is true that education and the accumulation of cultural capital can provide a route for individual social mobility, this is perfectly compatible with the production and maintenance of unequal social relations.

The delusions and disavowals of Hirsch's faith in the integrative power of literacy and education are particularly evident in his account of how the bonds of national community are established through a shared standard language. Of all the historical examples that tell this story differently, I shall cite just two. One is the account of the imposition of a standard French as the national language in the post-Revolutionary period offered by Renée Balibar.[17] This strategy allowed a *formal* equality at the same time as giving a new significance and value to the different dispositions towards the language. What had previously been simply regional and dialectal differences were now incorporated into new patterns of discrimination (between 'correct' and 'incorrect' usages, between 'polite' and 'vulgar' forms). Although we can accept Hirsch's insistence that the standard language is not simply the language of any one class fraction or region, nevertheless it is clear from Balibar's research that children of the bourgeoisie in their secondary schools were offered some understanding of how language works and so in some sense experienced it as their own. They learned that they had been speaking prose all their lives. In contrast to this, working-class pupils in the elementary schools established in the nineteenth century were instructed in the mechanical rules of 'grammar'. This school language, argues Balibar, was experienced as an external imposition, and also as an exclusion from a superior language and culture. These children learned that they didn't talk proper.

The other example is the fascinating story (told by Gauri Viswanathan) of how English literary studies had their origins as a technique of government in colonial India. As one administrator put it in 1838, 'The Natives must either be kept down by a sense of our power, or they must willingly submit from a conviction that we are more wise, more just, more humane, and more anxious to improve their condition than any other rulers they could have.' This is the context in which supposedly moralizing English texts became the objects of study for a class of translators, civil servants, and so forth. Even here, though, the power of literacy retained its ambivalence. C.E. Trevelyan, an influential member of the Council of Education, noted in 1853 that this strategy could not avoid the idea that the power and authority embodied in the provided texts might become accessible to those supposedly subordinated to them. Some of the educated natives, he observed, had an idea that 'we have gained everything by our superior knowledge; that it is this superiority which has enabled us to conquer India, and to keep it; and they want to put themselves as much as they can upon an equality with us.' *As much as they can* – the consequence of those limits was the formation of what Homi Bhabha, adapting V.S. Naipaul, has called 'mimic men'. This subaltern class takes on the values and mannerisms of the provided culture, but without them ever quite fitting: 'almost the same, but not white,' says Bhabha.[18]

The moral of these other histories of language, power and exclusion is that Hirsch misrecognizes national language and cultural literacy. They are never *only* means of healing social divisions and so of achieving economic efficiency and social justice: they always also produce cultural differences and evaluative hierarchies. Nevertheless, it is important not to underestimate or trivialize his desire for universality and community. Literacy is not just an individual capacity: it does play an important role in organizing law, citizenship and public life. So yes, Hirsch's account of reading remains too mechanical; yes, his List of information is a grotesque simplification of a culture's operative symbolic codes; yes, he disavows the patterns of difference and discrimination contained by the precarious 'identity' of a national community. But the problem of how to democratize literacy and culture remains.

It is therefore instructive to compare Hirsch's ideas with *The Primary Language Record: A Handbook for Teachers.* This was published in 1989 by the Inner London Education Authority's Centre for Language in Primary Education to accompany assessment procedures which have been endorsed by the National Curriculum English Subject Working Group. The authors of the *PLR* share Hirsch's aim of 'empowering' children, but they see literacy less in terms of securing access to a body of valued information than as the cultivation of an innate capacity. They do not fall into Hirsch's stereotyped image of naive Rousseauians standing back and letting children's natural aptitudes develop. On the contrary, the *PLR* can be read as a practical yet implicitly polemical alternative to Piagetian notions of individual development and maturation, one that draws instead on a Vygotskian notion of the social formation of cognitive abilities. This is why they promote the 'language-experience approach' to literacy, which 'stressed the importance of using children's first-hand experiences and natural interests in helping them to acquire and develop reading and writing skills'.[19] It is not so much the theoretical underpinnings of the *PLR* that I am interested in, however, as the techniques it recommends, and the knowledges and definitions these embody.

The *PLR*'s emphasis is on monitoring and recording what the handbook defines as 'significant aspects of language growth' in each child in exhaustive detail. The teacher's authority derives less from her role as representative of the literate culture than from her performance as interlocutor, scribe, confidante and guide. The pedagogic art lies in managing both the 'social and curriculum dimensions' of 'the learning environment', creating the contexts which will elicit the various linguistic performances the teacher is looking for. Drama is especially important as it allows children 'to use what they already know about the world (their understanding and experience of it) in an imagined context, and through it to explore issues and concepts important for them and the communities they live in'. Because she is 'working alongside children in creating imagined realities', drama also means that 'a teacher can change her status in the classroom, enabling children to talk with each other and with her in a way which is often difficult in the real life of the classroom, where the power relationships between adults and children are usually fixed.'[20]   If this account of the formation of the child, the exemplary role of the teacher, and the special claims of English and drama to be true to children's experience sounds familiar, that may be because here the *PLR* recalls an influential approach from the 1960s. This was lucidly expressed in John Dixon's *Growth through English* (1967).

> The taking on of dramatic roles, the dramatic encounter with new situations and with new possibilities of the self, is not something we *teach* children but something they bring to school for us to help them develop.... How can a teacher help pupils engaged in so personal a task to weigh up what has been achieved? All of us test the validity of what we have said by sensing how far others that we trust have shared our response. An English teacher tries to be a person to whom pupils turn

with that sense of trust. The sensitivity, honesty and tact of his response to what pupils say will confirm their half-formed certainties and doubts in what they have said.

The *PLR*'s strategies also recall a far longer tradition of popular education. It is impossible not to hear echoes of Kay-Shuttleworth's insistence on the importance of the 'sympathy of numbers', or David Stow's stress on the importance of the schoolmaster not only observing children at play in the playground – 'the arena on which their true character and dispositions are exhibited' – but also being willing on occasion to take part in their games so that 'they can, without fear, make him their confidant, unburden their minds, and tell him any little story, or mischievous occurrence'.[21]

This comparison suggests how the pastoral mode of power informs the *PLR*'s strategies and presuppositions: the demand on children to narrate and acknowledge their own experience, the appeal to norms and principles defined by educational psychology, and proposals for structured interviews about language and literacy with parents and pupils. The interviews with pupils, for example, are supposed to be 'a continuation of an already existing dialogue between child and teacher' in which it can 'be made clear to children that interests that exist beyond the confines of the school are not only relevant and valid in themselves, but also of great interest in discussions about their language/literacy development'. The summary of the conference becomes part of the archive of information about the individual pupil, and the flip side of indicating to children 'that what they say is being taken seriously' is that they take on a key role in their own supervision: they are required to take responsibility for their own formation and development. Once again, we are dealing with techniques for the inculcation of self-monitoring capacities.[22]

This is not to imply that the *PLR* approach has no educational value. It has clearly galvanized many primary teachers and provided a structure that children can often negotiate with considerable benefit. Its authors' commitment to the notion of English as emancipation, however, does tend to disavow the ambivalence of literacy. It is therefore legitimate to ask in what sense their methods prove more 'liberating' or 'empowering' than other pedagogic styles.

If advocates of this approach were to criticize Hirsch on the grounds that his endorsement of 'literate culture' disdains the experiences, languages and cultures of 'disadvantaged' children as deficient or inadequate, for example, the Hirschian might riposte that the misrecognition of social norms as innate capacities establishes a pathological model of those who do not conform to that pattern. If the progressive objects that Hirsch's strategy will not work because he misconceives unequal relations of power as a body of socially neutral information, the Hirschian could point out that the *PLR Handbook* consistently reduces 'the social' to questions of inter-personal relations. And this critic might go on to argue that whereas Hirsch's insistence on socialization into the literate national culture as a necessary 'second culture' at least opens up the possibility for a critical distance on experience, and so of individual mobility and cultural change, the progressive insistence that schools should 'value children's cultures, lives and experiences' entails a moral relativism that could be culturally quite conservative. There is often a tension between the progressives' desire for mobility and change, on the one hand, and their scruples about disturbing the claims and comforts of community, on the other. Theirs is not the Lyotardian idea of community as an always-to-be-achieved aspiration – as unknown – but the familiar notion of community as cultural baggage.

A left Hirschian (if such is possible) might therefore invoke Gramsci's injunction that the teacher 'must be aware of the contrast between the type of culture and society which he represents and the type of culture and society represented by his pupils, and conscious of his obligation to accelerate and regulate the child's formation in conformity with the former and in conflict with the latter'. As if to reinforce this principle, Gramsci's own biography could be cited as a salutary warning against the progressive tendency to disavow the power embodied in, and exercised through, language, literacy and education. Gramsci himself never made that mistake. Being the only Italian speaker in his village in Sardinia helped him to win a scholarship to Turin University in 1911, where he studied philology. He knew that there are many possible grammars or dialects – which may be equally valid *sub specie aeternitatis* – but he also insisted that the choice between them was always 'a political act'. The problem for him was not how to 'value' Sardinian peasant culture and dialect, but how to find forms of language that would contribute to the construction of a national-popular will. These are the same, somewhat Hirschian priorities evident in Gramsci's ideas about education. The starting point remains, to be sure, the culture and experience of the pupil, but the objective is change through the student's active and self-directed engagement with the skills and the often arduous disciplines of the school.[23]

If Sardinia in the early part of the century seems far away and long ago, similar questions arise from the educational career of another socialist intellectual closer to home. In *The Country and the City*, Raymond Williams acknowledges, again from his own experience, the claims of community or, to use his word, settlement: 'an identification with the people among whom we grew up; an attachment to the place, the landscape, in which we first lived and learned to see.' The value of this first idea of settlement is 'positive and unquestioned'. He didn't need anyone to reaffirm it or idealize it for him, even though he 'had to move out for an education and to go on with a particular kind of work'.

> I know, in just that sense, what neighbourhood means, and what is involved in separation and leaving. But I know, also, why people have had to move, why so many moved in my own family. So that I then see the idealization of settlement, in its ordinary literary-historical version, as an insolent indifference to most people's needs.[24]

I am not accusing the *PLR* of such insolent idealization; its authors are too sophisticated and politically sensitive for that. But these examples underline an important lesson of which Hirsch's crusade is a flawed and inadvertent reminder: that culture is never something we own, it remains always elusively other. This shifts the criteria for what constitutes a democratic education away from an emphasis on community or experience or identity, and towards the terms on which students participate in social and cultural transactions. For Hirsch, submission to established cultural norms is a precondition for autonomous participation later. The *PLR* authors concentrate instead on involving children in the educational possibilities of self-formation here and now.

If Hirsch thus overemphasizes universalizing modes of power and the *PLR* individuating modes, they both share an overinflated notion of what literacy can deliver. If only we could get literacy right, they imply, that will produce (for Hirsch) or reveal (for *PLR*) citizens who would exercise their talents and innate creative abilities to the full. It would also ensure the full flowering of a democratic culture. And at that point, the debate usually congeals into stale oppositions between individuation and socialization, progressivism and traditionalism, liberal education and vocationalism, emancipation and social control.

Refunctioning Literacy

It is to avoid that sclerosis that I have been trying to rephrase the question of what democratization might mean in relation to higher education and literacy. I argue that neither human nature nor an idealized national community offers a plausible starting point for a democratic education. I accept both the impossibility of a universal educated public and yet also the tragi-comic inescapability of participating in collective relations of power. That recognition at least gets rid of images of the full development and expression of individual talents being thwarted and deformed by the dull compulsion of wage labour and the oppressions of everyday life. Accept the ambivalence of participation and agency – we are always both *subjects of* and *subject to* – and it is impossible to imagine the exercise of liberty as a psychotic escape from relations of power. Instead, it becomes an invitation or an obligation to act on the basis that the rules of the game can be changed *while it is being played,* however rigged the game may be in favour of some players and against others.[25]

From this point of view, education is revealed as both an instance of participation in the social and the symbolic, and also as a threshold to further participation in the labour market and civil society. The next task, then, is to identify those authoritative discourses and practices that define the terms of this participation, and to consider how they might be organized so as to enhance their democratic or improvisatory aspects. Some notion of cultural and social literacy must be central, although not Hirsch's. To underline how my version would differ from his, I would place a *critical vocationalism* at the heart of mine.

Here a measure of cynicism is certainly justified. Since the mid-1970s, under both Labour and Conservative governments, most vocational initiatives for young people in the United Kingdom, like the Youth Training Scheme (YTS), the Technical, Vocational and Educational Initiative (TVEI) and their successors, have been unimaginative and incoherent. They have had less to do with developing the technical skills and intellectual competences needed for industrial regeneration than with socializing unemployed and/or low skilled workers into the behavioural imperatives that employers find reassuring in terms of workplace discipline and which politicians see as prerequisites for an enterprise culture. As one astute observer has noted, vocationalism over recent years has generally turned out to to be 'an ideology of production regulating education rather than an educational ideology servicing production'. Questions about the democratization of either work or education have been nowhere on this agenda.[26]

In contrast to this disciplinary vocationalism, a critical vocationalism would begin by asking what concepts, knowledges and intellectual skills would be necessary for understanding how industries and economies work, in order to develop the potential for autonomy in the shaping of a career.

What would be the economic and social benefits of such education? Britain's poor, and declining, industrial performance is frequently attributed, in part at least, to the lack of a workforce trained to high levels of skill, adaptability and innovation. These characteristics are necessary, it is argued, for those 'flexible-system' production strategies that will increasingly have to displace low-skill-based mass production if more of British manufacturing industry is to become competitive. The failure to make this transition has been both a cause and a consequence of the low levels both of post-sixteen participation in full-time education and of firm-based training. Firms that think in terms of minimizing costs and unrestrained price competition are unwilling to invest in training: it is cheaper to do without skilled workers or, if they are essential, to poach those already trained elsewhere. This exposes again the inefficiency of the market in securing the conditions for its own prosperity. To rectify these shortcomings and to bump-start the economy into a 'high-skills equilibrium' would require a quite new commitment to consultation, co-operation and consensus not only between firms at local and regional level, but also within firms. The aim is an industrial public sphere in which the leading actors would be less individual citizens and workers than firms, public agencies, unions and employers' federations negotiating decisions about training, equal opportunities, investment, the impact of production on the environment, and so forth.[27]

In that sort of market context, a general education would have to teach some understanding of the complex technological, economic and industrial systems that structure the organization of production and the exercise of power in modern Western societies. Otherwise it would be producing students who are, in a partial but practical way, illiterate. Equally, any vocationalism that was not critical – that taught only mechanical skills and deference, that ignored the determinants and consequences of decisions and practices, and that did not require students to think about them would be inefficient and inappropriate. Vocationalism would then no longer refer just to the provision of job-specific apprenticeships or 'relevant' courses for low academic achievers. It would have to address as a priority the potential role of educational institutions in creating a skilled, informed and participatory workforce as a precondition for industrial democracy as well as economic effectiveness.[28]

Given the utopian note that can sometimes be heard in the socialist advocacy of flexible specialization or post-Fordism, it is important to remember that, in British firms at least, the new opportunities are more often being used to deskill, divide and control the workforce in the name of an aggressive and unimaginative managerialism than to enhance its intellectual and practical capacities. Even if the more autonomous styles of work were to be established, they would probably apply to an elite of permanent full-time workers at the expense of a growing body of less secure workers, often working part-time or on job-shares, or else as self-employed subcontractors. Also, of course, they depend on gross – and growing – inequalities in the international division of labour. These dangers, however, do not constitute a truth that exposes the myths of the Enterprise Culture or reveals flexible specialization to be the latest and subtlest of capitalism's protean forms of exploitation. The point is rather to perceive the ambivalences in these changes in the social relations of work, and to realize that they define the limits of any possible exercise of liberty – that is, the critical reflection on their contingency.

This perspective thus makes it possible to understand why, in some accounts of flexible specialization and/or post-Fordism, there is an almost uncanny echo of the principal condition that Alasdair MacIntyre defined as necessary for the existence of an educated public. This was that critical discussion on shared terms should be a feature of the roles and functions into which students are socialized, and it is the potential for autonomy that this creates which democrats welcome. Given my scepticism about the opposition between socialization and individuation on which that image is based, however, it seems equally logical to read this potential for autonomy as the emergence of new techniques for managing a workforce through the ascription of identities as independent, self-fulfilling workers. The gist of the management bible of the 1980s, Peters and Waterman's *In Search of Excellence*, is that the ability to grasp and use people's aspirations, irrationality and self-motivation is the secret of management success. Flexibility, adaptability, experimentation and informality are the buzz words, backed up by a pop-psychological imagery of people as self-realizing and self-fulfilling. New techniques of capital accumulation are thus accompanied by new techniques for inculcating self-monitoring and self-managing capacities.[29]

Even if flexible specialization were to become the norm, there is no reason to suppose that greed and incompetence would suddenly disappear. Under any foreseeable democratic socialism, labour markets will continue to operate, and they will be characterized by degrees of inequality and antagonism. The question is, how might education and training help to maximize the possibilities for autonomy and contest the inequitable and discriminatory practices of employment and management that exist at present? This implies neither the old socialist dream of liberating the full capacities of man through labour, nor its neo-liberal equivalent of entrepreneurial self-fulfilment. Critical vocationalism is more concerned with the institutional structures and procedures through which the negotiations and conflicts of the social – and here specifically of production, work and employment – are staged.

This approach to vocationalism as part of an expanded literacy thus focuses on the educational conditions necessary for the existence of a radical democracy: what knowledges, skills and resources would citizens need in order to be able to participate effectively in its dialogue and negotiations? If the ability to reflect critically on social roles and functions is one, perhaps we should look again at the other conditions for an educated public, which MacIntyre identifies; that is, canonical cultural references, mutually accepted standards of authority, and shared modes of argumentation and justification.

Defining the political community in terms of a nationalist assimilationism was, of course, central to the initial strategy of the National Curriculum. Here the literate or educated public was to be identified in terms of the cultural *content* of the curriculum. To qualify for membership is to be at home with *this* form of language, *this* selection of books, *this* Christianity, *this* heritage – Kenneth Baker's List as tempered (or subverted, some would claim) by the working parties of the National Curriculum Council, in this case, rather than Hirsch's List. However offensive or dotty such inventories may be, the idea of an educated public does presuppose some shared points of reference. To deny certain groups access to valued cultural forms is one way in which cultural inequalities are reproduced. That is why the demand for such access has often been a characteristic of working-class and feminist educational movements. They have realized that what is at stake in debates about content and access is the authority embodied in and instituted by cultural traditions. The problem is that in a multicultural society, there can be no one centre of authority – although that is the premiss of most official educational multiculturalism, which incorporates other cultures and traditions only as long as they do not trouble established norms and categories. To define literacy as one, and only one, set of cultural luggage is to set in place effective mechanisms of differentiation and discrimination rather than of universal inclusiveness.

The challenge is therefore to decouple the identification of shared cultural referents – the terms in which community is imagined –

from the retroactive legitimacy bestowed on them by traditions of nationality or ethnicity. However much we are taught that they are handed down from past generations, such canons are present inventions that identify 'us' and differentiate 'us' from 'them'. What multiculturalism requires, if taken seriously, is to displace this version of community as always already fixed in favour of the idea of community as unknown, uncentred, always to be constructed in the process of dialogue and self-naming. That aspiration, I think, lies behind this description of the range of activities that might now make up English teaching in a London secondary school:

> A first year class might be discussing cultural assumptions and narrative forms through the reading of folk-tales and fairy stories, using simple deconstruction strategies. A second year class might be considering the publicity and marketing of a class reader or its adaptation for television while a third year group plan and draft pieces for a poetry anthology to be used in primary schools. In the fourth year, language itself might be under discussion with pupils exploring regional and historical shifts in dialect. Fifth years might be involved in Literature Open Studies; exploring the genre of crime fiction or comparing a Hardy novel to a work of contemporary popular fiction. In the sixth form GCSE mature students might be analysing the representation of children in television advertisements. CPVE [Certificate of Pre-Vocational Education] students might be writing an account of their work experience. An A-level class might be reading a Hemingway short story from the perspective of a number of critical stances; Leavisite, post-structuralist, feminist, psychoanalytical.

Here it is recognized that the content of the syllabus is provisional and always subject to change and negotiation. What matters is the strategy governing its selection: not just the question of who gets access to what, but above all the emphasis on concepts, perspectives and semiotic skills. Literary language is treated as one discursive genre among others. Texts are set in their historical and institutional contexts to show how the production of meaning is linked to the exercise of power. Students are offered a critical familiarity with the techniques of different media, and are confronted with a variety of intellectual frameworks for making sense of themselves and the social world.[30]

This version of literacy is restricted neither to a familiarity with the best that has supposedly been thought and written, nor to the exercise of an innate aesthetic capacity, nor to the acknowledgement of an essential experience. Nevertheless, it does still refer, implicitly at least, to a kernel of shared values and beliefs: empathy, sensitivity to difference, tolerance and mutual respect. From this point of view, it does not matter whether or not you have read the same books as your fellow citizens, whether you share their religious or political convictions, or even speak the same language. But you do have to accept the same rules of the game for political negotiation. The minimal requirement for membership of an educated public would then be a shared definition of what is at issue, and agreement about how to disagree.

This anyway is the premiss of Amy Gutmann's liberal argument. She makes the assertion, for example, that 'children must learn not just to *behave* in accordance with authority but to *think* critically about authority if they are to live up to the democratic ideal of sharing political sovereignty as citizens.'[31] Although that encapsulates forcefully the version of liberty I have been arguing for, Gutmann's formulation also indicates some of its limits. Her commitment to critical thought is predicated on the acceptance of the 'democratic ideal' as the only conceivable outcome of the interrogation. Gutmann does not seem to allow for the possibility of critical perspectives incommensurable with this axiom and so, in effect, pre-empts the outcome of the dialogue. She may substitute the democratic ideal for the enlightened monarch, but in effect she reasserts Kant's paradoxical principle of *intellectual* autonomy within strict *political* limits: 'Argue as much as you will, and about what you will, only obey!' I would give this a slightly different gloss: although democratic sovereignty may be an 'empty place', the exercise of liberty is bounded by the technologies of the social. Where, then, in 'our' post-colonial democracy, does that leave those who – whether by alternative affiliation or by exclusion – do not share Gutmann's ideal? To seek universally shared values or dispositions is once again to highlight the experience of division.

This aporia suggests that the literacy adequate to a radical, heterogeneous democracy might need to be driven neither by a normative identity nor a performative political ideal, but by the principle and skills of cultural translation, the ability to negotiate across incommensurable traditions. Alasdair MacIntyre has suggested what might be involved: .

> the only rational way for the adherents of any tradition to approach intellectually, culturally, and linguistically alien rivals is one that allows for the possibility that in one or more areas the other may be rationally superior to it in respect precisely of that in the alien tradition which it cannot comprehend. The claim made within each tradition that the presently established beliefs shared by the adherents of that tradition are true entails a denial that this is in fact going to happen in respect of those beliefs, but it is the possibility of this nonetheless happening which ... gives point to the assertion of truth and provides assertions of truth and falsity with a content which makes them other than even idealized versions of assertions of warranted assertability. The existence of large possibilities of untranslatability and therefore of potential threats to the cultural, linguistic, social, and rational hegemony of one's own tradition, either in some particular area or overall, is therefore more and other than a threat. Only those whose tradition allows for the possibility of its hegemony being put in question can have rational warrant for asserting such a hegemony. And only those traditions whose adherents recognize the possibility of untranslatability into their own language-in-use are able to reckon adequately with that possibility.[32]

Although this does presuppose an effective political pluralism, it entails neither a corporatism that takes interest groups and cultural identities at face value, nor an 'anything-goes' relativism. Instead, it sees the institution of authority – or hegemony – as definitive of a tradition, while acknowledging that such authority is always limited by the terms of that tradition and so provisional and open to question. This is therefore the exact opposite of that version of tradition as absolute and unquestionable imposed through the National Curriculum. In its insistence on the recursiveness of reason and its scepticism towards foundationalism, MacIntyre's account of tradition and translation attempts to achieve the same balance between the desire for justice and the desire for the unknown that characterizes Lyotard's aspiration to community.

Does this suggest that we should try to desacralize literacy, to rid it of encrusted cultural accretions and interpret it purely as those skills and competences necessary for interpreting differences, for analysing information, for reaching decisions and for acting on them? This is an attractive option in that it implies a practical orientation for teaching, and opens up the possibility of negotiating criteria of accountability; that is, establishing 'performance indicators' for institutions and teachers which would at the same time be 'entitlements' for students.[33] This could respect the various interests in the process of schooling without falling back into the lazy imagery of consumerism. In the end, however, it only partly sidesteps the problem. Techniques and skills are as embedded in intellectual and cultural traditions as values and artefacts. Society cannot be rendered transparent. Our fantasmatic investment in identities and communities ensures the continuation of a social imaginary bounded by the sacred and the abject. That aspect of schooling cannot be so hygienically packaged as rights and entitlements.

Democracy, Authority, Participation

There are no universally agreed criteria for what constitutes a social and cultural literacy. It follows that the type of educated public required by an Enlightenment theory of participatory democracy cannot exist. Today, that idea of a public lingers on as part of a republican myth of the Ideal City. To counter its seductive but dangerous appeal, I have attempted to rearticulate some of its main themes in a new register.

In political terms, Amy Gutmann suggests, the question posed by a democratic theory of education is this: 'Who should have the authority to shape the education of future citizens?' That may seem uncontroversial enough, but it marks a radical break from the Rousseauian notion of a community that is both author and subject of a General Will. A democratic theory, Gutmann admits, cannot offer practical solutions to all the problems that afflict educational institutions. That is why she poses education as a question, the question of an authority that is always in question. The aim should be to devise ways of resolving – or even of discussing – those problems in ways that are compatible with democratic values: questions about who gets access to what forms of knowledge, on

169

what terms, and with what likely consequences.[34]

Rather than delivering confident programmes for educational reform, this approach raises the question of what popular involvement and professional accountability would mean once you accept Lefort's principles that in a heterogeneous and dissensual democracy 'what is instituted never becomes established' and the identity of the people 'will constantly be open to question'. If you reject the fictional 'parent' of populist conservatism, the progressive orthodoxies of emancipation and self-realization, and also the cynicism of aimless reformism, what is left is the agonistic dialogue as itself constituting authority in a democratic community. Its point of cohesion would be neither the myth of a shared descent nor the claims of a General Will, but the aspiration to self-determined social reproduction. Rather than wishing away conflicts, inequalities and incommensurabilities, this approach should at least create a space for marginal and emergent voices in defining terms and setting limits to authority in debates about education.[35]

The emphasis on norms of cultural authority as necessary but always subject to critical reflection has far-reaching implications for the discourses and practices of educational institutions. In looking at pedagogy and the curriculum, I have shown, first, *how* authoritative concepts, categories and values are embodied in the routines of education, and, second, the *terms* on which students can engage with them. This suggests that the aim should not be to fix the curriculum once and for all, whether to consolidate a cultural tradition or to provoke total social transformation. Rather, its content should remain always under review and adaptable to changes in knowledge or in society.

This restless experimentalism also entails a reconceptualization of the subjects at whom education is targeted. Here the logic follows Lefort's account of how the *position* of 'the people' authorizes democratic sovereignty, and yet – and so – cannot be a position occupied by any person, group or party. Similarly, the subject of democracy is a contentless abstraction, not a psychological profile. To be a citizen is to be ascribed a certain status, it is not to be a particular type of person. And yet, of course, modern education has consistently been allotted the task of sustaining social relations by creating psychologically adjusted, productive, enterprising and patriotic citizens. It is that attempt to reconcile the split between the pedagogic demands of citizenship and the enigmatic particularity of agency and subjectivity which, following Freud, I take to be impossible.

It is also undesirable. Education should not be about the engineering of human souls. Instead, I have tried to sketch some of the political principles, modes of conduct and individual capacities that education might seek to institute in the process of creating and extending a radically democratic public sphere.

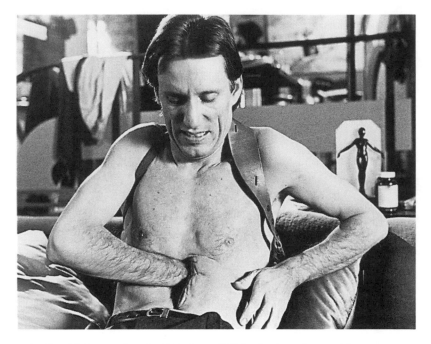

In David Cronenberg's *Videodrome* (1983), the hero has a videocassette thrust into the wound that appears in his stomach. 'Is it not commonplace nowadays to say that the forces of man have already entered into a relation with the forces of information technology and their third-generation machines which together create something other than man, indivisible "man-machine" systems?' (Gilles Deleuze, *Foucault*, p. 89)

CODA

The Happiest Time . . .

In my Introduction, I suggested that the *Bildungsroman* provides a clue to the importance of education in Western modernity. Both the symbolic form of the novel and the social apparatus of the school are concerned with the conduct of life within a field structured by forces of power and authority. They both narrate the self's formation as a conflict between the supposedly *natural* dispositions of youth and what are experienced as the *constraints* of society. This narrative has been institutionalized not only by novelists, but also by psychologists, philosophers and generations of school teachers. It continues to structure those familiar educational debates in which 'traditionalists' defend the demands and comforts of civilization, whatever the costs of individual adaptation, against 'progressives' who celebrate self-creation and the possibilities of transformation.

It is because of this tenacious and disabling after-life that I have argued so insistently on the need to ditch this post-Rousseauian narrative of socialization. Let me illustrate why one last time by juxtaposing two exemplary, though very different, modernist figures: Flaubert the novelist and John Dewey the educationalist.

Many contemporary critics were scandalized by the bleakness and cynicism of Flaubert's conclusion to his *Sentimental Education* (1869). The hero, Frédéric Moreau, has an inheritance which had allowed him to move freely through different social spheres, sites and scenes, rather like a detective without a case. He has witnessed the historical turmoil of Paris in 1848, become part of its Bohemian society, and experienced a grand passion. What has he learned from all this? Not

173

maturity, it seems, if that means the mandated and regulated autonomy of the well-adapted citizen. It is not even that self-determination is being postponed as a possibility for the future. Indeterminacy has become an end in itself.

In the novel's penultimate scene, he is visited by Madame Arnoux, the woman he has loved for twenty years. Given a final chance to consummate the relationship, to realize his fantasy, he responds with irritation and a hint of repugnance: 'And partly out of prudence and partly to avoid degrading his ideal, he turned on his heel and started rolling a cigarette.' In the final episode of the novel, Frédéric reminisces with his old schoolfriend Deslauriers about their youth. The conversation turns to an adolescent escapade in which they visited the local brothel on the edge of their town:

It was during the holidays of 1837 that they had been to the Turkish woman's house.

This was the name usually given to a woman who was really called Zoraïde Turc; and many people actually believed that she was a Mohammedan from Turkey. This added to the romantic appeal of her establishment, which was situated on the river bank, behind the ramparts. Even at the height of summer there was a shade around her house, which was recognizable by a bowl of goldfish next to a pot of mignonette on a windowsill. Girls in white dressing-gowns, with rouge on their cheeks and long ear-rings, used to tap on the windowpanes as one passed, and in the evening they would stand on the doorstep singing softly in husky voices.

This haunt of perdition enjoyed a remarkable reputation in the whole district. People referred to it by euphemisms: 'You know where I mean ... a certain street ... below the Bridges.' It made the farmers' wives of the neighbourhood tremble for their husbands; well-to-do women feared its influence on their maids, because the sub-prefect's cook had been caught there; and it was, of course, the secret obsession of every adolescent.

One Sunday, when everybody was at Vespers, Frédéric and Deslauriers, having previously had their hair curled, picked some flowers in Madame Moreau's garden, and then went out by the gate leading to the fields. After a long detour through the vineyards, they came back by the Pêcherie and slipped into the Turkish woman's house, still holding their big nosegays.

Frédéric presented his, like a lover to his betrothed. But the heat of the day, fear of the unknown, a sort of remorse, and also the very pleasure of seeing at a single glance so many women at his disposal affected him so powerfully that he turned deathly pale, and stood still, without saying a word. The girls all burst out laughing, amused by his embarrassment; thinking they were making fun of him, he fled, and as Frédéric had the money, Deslauriers had no choice but to follow him.

They were seen coming out. This caused a local scandal which was still remembered three years later.

They told one another the story at great length, each supplementing the other's recollections; and when they had finished:

'That was the happiest time we ever had,' said Frédéric.

'Yes, perhaps you're right. That was the happiest time we ever had,' said Deslauriers.[1]

Moreau recognizes himself as a subject of desire, as subject to his desires. 'Too sentimental', according to Deslauriers, he remains under the tutelage of conventionally banal fantasies. Madame Arnoux is idealized only as long as she is unattainable. The exotic transgressions offered by the 'Turkish woman' are a parody of Orientalism. Judging by Moreau's conduct, however, these fantasies produce neither the obsessive disciplines of Sade's libertinage nor the vicissitudes of abstinence or fidelity. Instead, a 'fear of the unknown' and 'a sort of remorse' make him shy away, even if that makes him appear so contemptible or farcical as to explode the very authority of the *Bildungsroman*.

One of the most attractive features of John Dewey's work is its unfussy anti-essentialism. In human beings, he sees no Rousseauian nature to be repressed or liberated, and so rejects any idea of a 'fixed, ready-made, finished self'. The state represents neither the origin nor the end-point of power. What Dewey sees are historically specific and necessarily 'experimental' arrangements of social institutions, shaped as much by the residue of adjustments to past circumstances as by the present dialogue between different 'publics', 'interests' and 'actors'. It is this historicity that makes constant critical examination and reconstruction essential. The aim should be to help the people on whom these institutions operate. His guiding principle is an ideal of democratic community, even if that ideal is incapable of realization. ('Democracy in this sense is not

175

a fact and never will be,' Dewey acknowledges.)[2]

This emphasis on contingency, reflection and mutability has led Richard Rorty to declare that Dewey not only pioneered the sort of genealogical reflection on the present undertaken by Foucault, but that he went further and did it better. Both, says Rorty, wanted to make philosophy useful to those, in Foucault's phrase, 'whose fight is located in the fine meshes of the webs of power'. The advantage of Dewey is that 'his vocabulary allows room for unjustifiable hope, and an ungroundable but vital sense of human solidarity.'[3]

Rorty's is a provocative conclusion, but questionable. It is true that Dewey shows no nostalgia for a normative General Will, and that he does not justify his prescriptions by reference to epistemological norms or fixed utopian visions. Nevertheless, he does judge the value and efficacy of hope and solidarity by reference to the pragmatic ideal of 'social democracy' and a scientifically based practical reasoning. That is, means should not only be judged by ideal ends, but ends should also be matched to existing means: the search for the means by which the ideal might be realized would thus act back on the representation of the ideal. However provisional and experimental this process, the criteria are more solidly grounded and justified, and less negotiable, than Rorty implies. For Dewey, democracy is not a choice of one among other 'principles of associated life'. The aspiration to harmony and resolution through critical reflection represents 'the idea of community life itself': it is by definition the only possible ideal. Only through communication and interaction on this basis can diverse and conflicting interests, beliefs and desires find avenues of development and growth.[4]

Although in general the idea of community operates as a horizon in Dewey's thought along the same lines as in Lyotard's, he sometimes slips into a lapsarian imagery of what constitutes good and effective community. In *The Public and its Problems* (1927), for example, he envisages the revitalization of public life through the multiplication of publics and the creation of a community of communities. The building blocks in this task were to be face-to-face participation and debate:

> Unless local communal life can be restored, the public cannot adequately solve its most urgent problem; to find and identify itself. But

if it be re-established, it will manifest a fullness, variety and freedom of possession and enjoyment of meanings and goods unknown in the contiguous associations of the past. For it will be alive and flexible as well as stable, responsive to the complex and world-wide scene in which it is enmeshed. While local, it will not be isolated.

This nostalgia for the small-town meeting is quite different from anything in Foucault's political writings. It provides another reason for my scepticism about Rorty's claim that the difference between Dewey and Foucault is '*merely* one of tone – an ingenuous Anglo-Saxon pose as opposed to a self-dramatizing Continental one'.[5]

Rorty is right to stress the importance of tone, nevertheless, because it is at this level that the tension between a revived communitarianism and a sometimes nihilistic critique is most clearly registered in post-modern cultural thought. Those different accents are already evident for example, in Dewey's sometimes rather earnest optimism and Flaubert's unsentimental irony as he deconstructs the narrative of self-formation and mature autonomy in his portrait of Moreau.

Moreau represents a man who can afford independence, and who buys it at the cost of what Dewey would see as the possibilities for fulfilment offered by engagement with a wider community. In pursuing his aimless pleasures, Moreau in practice relates to his 'self' as something narrow, trivial, transient and exclusive. Dewey's alternative is to imagine a self which, although always unfinished, is none the less capacious enough to embrace the interests of other people, and permanent and significant enough to flourish in an environment sustained by shared values and co-operative action. Is there not a danger, though, that this damning audit of Moreau's egotism might ultimately authorize the social tyranny of enforced virtue? Not for Dewey, because he would see that line of argument as premised on a misconceived belief in 'the naked individual' for whom 'all associations are foreign to his nature and rights save as they [proceed] from his own voluntary choice, and [guarantee] his own private ends'. In Moreau's blasé detachment, Dewey might well have diagnosed a lack of the moral education that would make him more responsibly aware of the effects on himself and others of his sentimental pursuits.[6]

Flaubert's conclusion, of course, is that such moral education doesn't work, or at least that it doesn't work for all of us all of the time. It is this comic fact that some contemporary communitarians, in many ways the heirs of Dewey, find it hard to accept. When they tut-tut at free-riders and wag their fingers at civic backsliders, they forget the warnings given by Kant and Freud about the impossibility of education and government. When they try to quarantine the egotism of a Moreau (or any of us) within a private sphere that should not impinge on public obligations, they are attempting to establish a *cordon sanitaire* around the solidarity and authority of their communal 'we'. That is to disavow my repeated argument that such authority can only be enacted even as its apparent solidity and universality are erased in the singularity and performativity of agency.

What might all this mean for the practical business of education and politics? I am certainly not suggesting that policy programmes can be derived from Flaubert's cynicism or from Foucault's genealogical reflections on the present. But as the examples of radical communitarianism or Rorty's cosy liberal conversations underline, it always remains important to deflate claims to authority – claims to speak and, even more, claims to *speak for* – as they threaten to become too monological, too universalistic and so too exclusive. It is therefore especially important to heed different, marginal, abnormal and transgressive voices that question the 'we' of political dialogue and the 'I' of agency.

It is this move, both sublime and populist, that has led to a curious feature of post-modernism: that is, recording as signs of hope the old Enlightenment terrors about the instability of human boundaries evident in the monster, the vampire and the robot. In Foucault's dismantling of the Classical and Modern forms of Man, for example, Gilles Deleuze sees a prelude to some new, as yet mute and unnameable form of what it is to be a social actor that is slouching into being. It appears to us still monstrous: a hybrid being whose Third Coming will be formed within still emergent technologies of subjectivization. Yet Donna Haraway is positively optimistic about the prospect. Treating Foucault's bio-politics as 'a flaccid premonition of cyborg politics', she sees no reason why those marginalized by the earlier forms and finitudes of Man should feel either regret or terror at their passing. Instead, she wants them to celebrate this monstrous future with its possibilities of 'both building and destroying machines, identities, categories, relationships, spaces, stories'.[7]

This suggests not only a new political ecology, but also a new style of political judgement. Could this accommodate both Flaubert's unflinching comic eye and Dewey's radical pragmatism – especially given that the tension between the two cannot be resolved or transcended? This sense of rational judgement as particularistic and recursive would mean jettisoning the complacent optimism of 'human solidarity', the irrationality of appeals to 'human nature' and an epic conception of History as the long march towards Utopia. It calls instead for the sustained critique of regimes of truth, the patient and practical reform of existing institutions, and yet also a political imagination, which, so far, looks more than anything like a witty and subversive science fiction.

NOTES

Introduction: Well-Regulated Liberty

1. Sigmund Freud, *The Standard Edition of the Complete Psychological Works*, vol. 23, ed. James Strachey, London, 1953–66, p. 248; Immanuel Kant, *Education*, Michigan, 1960, p. 12.

2. This formulation of the pedagogic and the performative I owe to Homi Bhabha. See his 'DissemiNation: Time, Narrative, and the Margins of the Modern Nation', in H. Bhabha, ed., *Nation and Narration*, London, 1990, pp. 297–9. On the formation of citizenship, see Nikolas Rose, 'Governing the Enterprising Self', paper for the conference *The Values of the Enterprise Culture*, University of Lancaster, September 1989; and *Governing the Soul: The Shaping of the Private Self*, London, 1990.

3. Michel de Certeau, *The Practice of Everyday Life*, Berkeley, 1984, p. xv.

4. Kant, *Education*, pp. 7, 28; 'What is Enlightenment?', in *Philosophical Writings*, ed. Ernst Behler, New York, 1986, p. 269.

5. Jean-Jacques Rousseau, *The Social Contract*, trans. Maurice Cranston, Harmondsworth, 1968, pp. 64–5; Carole Pateman, *The Problem of Political Obligation: A Critique of Liberal Theory*, Cambridge, 1985, p. 143; Rousseau, *Emile*, trans. Barbara Foxley, London, 1911, p. 217.

6. Rousseau, *Emile*, pp. 7, 40.

7. Ibid., pp. 9, 281–2, 84–5, 56. On this version of authority, see Claude Lefort, *The Political Forms of Modern Society*, Cambridge, 1986, pp. 211–14. On symbolic identification, Slavoj Žižek, *The Sublime Object of Ideology*, London, 1989, p. 105.

8. Ernst Cassirer, *Rousseau, Kant and Goethe*, New York, 1963, p. 9; William E. Connolly, *Political Theory and Modernity*, Oxford, 1988, pp. 57–8.

9. My account of the *Bildungsroman* draws on Franco Moretti, *The Way of the World: The* Bildungsroman *in European Culture*, London, 1987; see also the review by Graham Murdock, 'Imagining Modernity: Moretti on the *Bildungsroman*', *New Formations*, no. 6, 1988.

10. On the importance of adultery as a theme, see Tony Tanner, *Adultery in the Novel: Contract and Transgression*, Baltimore and London, 1979.

11. Schiller's *On the Aesthetic Education of Man*, cited in Ian Hunter, *Culture and Government: The Emergence of Literary Education*, London, 1988, pp. 184–5, 79.

12. Rousseau, *Emile*, pp. 321, 322, 328; Mary Wollstonecraft, *Vindication of the Rights of Woman*, Harmondsworth, 1982, pp. 81–3. My reading of Wollstonecraft draws on Cora Kaplan, *Sea Changes: Culture and Feminism*, London, 1986; and David Held, *Models of Democracy*, Cambridge, 1987, pp. 79–85.

13. Marquis de Sade, *Philosophy in the Bedroom*, in Richard Seaver and Austryn Wainhouse, eds, *The Marquis de Sade*, New York, 1965, p. 208. See also Connolly, *Political Theory and Modernity*, pp. 74–5. My account of Sade's relationship to Rousseau draws heavily on his 'First Interlude: Hobbes, Rousseau and the Marquis de Sade', in *Political Theory and Modernity*.

14. Connolly, *Political Theory and Modernity*, p. 78.

15. Rose, *Governing the Soul*, p. 7.

16. See Valerie Walkerdine, 'Developmental Psychology and the Child-centred Pedagogy', in Julian Henriques, Wendy Hollway, Cathy Urwin, Couze Venn and Valerie Walkerdine, *Changing the Subject*, London, 1984, pp. 169–73; and 'It's Only Natural: Rethinking Child-centred Pedagogy', in AnnMarie Wolpe and James Donald, eds, *Is There Anyone Here from Education?*, London, 1983.

17. Michel Foucault, 'The Subject and Power', in Herbert L. Dreyfus and Paul Rabinow, *Michel Foucault: Beyond Structuralism and Hermeneutics*, Brighton, 1982, pp. 221–2.

18. I have deliberately chosen these examples from books I admire: Ken Jones's perceptive critique of Thatcherite education policy, *Right Turn: The Conservative Revolution in Education*, London, 1989, p. 187; and Gregor McLennan's thorough-going critique of many of the positions I present here, *Marxism, Pluralism and Beyond*, Cambridge, 1989, p. 157.

19. Bhabha, 'DissemiNation', p. 297.

20. Ibid., p. 292.

21. Primarily Ian Hunter and Nikolas Rose: this debate underlines my indebtedness to their work.

1. Beacons of the Future

1. Michel Foucault, *Power/Knowledge: Selected Interviews and Other Writings*, ed. Colin Gordon, London, 1980, p. 102.

2. See, for example, Ian Hunter, *Culture and Government: The Emergence of Literary Education*, London, 1988, p. 163 and p. 125.

3. Horner, cited in Andy Green, *Education and State Formation: The Rise of Education Systems in England, France and the USA*, London, 1990, p. 251. Kay-Shuttleworth, cited in Brian Simon, *Studies in the History of Education, vol. 1: The Two Nations and the Educational Structure, 1780–1870*, London, 1960, p. 338; see also Hunter, *Culture and Government*, p. 56. On moral environmentalism, see Lucy Bland

and Frank Mort, 'Look Out for the "Good Time" Girl', in *Formations of Nation and People*, London, 1984, p. 132; and Frank Mort, *Dangerous Sexualities: Medico-moral Politics in England since 1830*, London, 1987.

4. 'The nightmare journey' is Bland and Mort's striking image, p. 133; Kay-Shuttleworth, cited in Bland and Mort,*Formatims*, p. 134; and Hunter, *Culture and Government*, pp. 55–6. On the child and the family, see Jacques Donzelot, *The Policing of Families*, London, 1979.

5. See Jeffrey Weeks, *Sex, Politics and Society: The Regulation of Sexuality since 1800*, London, 1981, ch. 7.

6. Nikolas Rose, 'The Psychological Complex: Mental Measurement and Social Administration', *Ideology and Consciousness*, no. 5, 1979, pp. 24, 26. On *Dracula* and eugenics, see Daniel Pick, '"Terrors of the Night": *Dracula* and "Degeneration" in the Late Nineteenth Century', *Critical Quarterly*, vol. 30, no. 4, 1988, p. 75; also Pick, *Faces of Degeneration: A European Disorder, c. 1848–c. 1918,* Cambridge, 1990.

7. See David A. Reeder, 'Predicaments of City Children: Late Victorian and Edwardian Perspectives on Education and Urban Society', in Reeder, ed., *Urban Education in the Nineteenth Century*, London, 1977, p. 78; Anna Davin, '"Mind that You Do as You Are Told": Reading Books for Board School Girls, 1870–1902', *Feminist Review*, no. 2, 1979; John Ahier, *Industry, Children and the Nation: An Analysis of National Identity in School Textbooks*, Lewes, 1988.

8. Reeder, *Urban Education*, p. 81; Brian Simon, *Studies in the History of Education, vol. 2: Education and the Labour Movement*, London, 1965, pp. 156–8.

9. Sydney Webb, 'Lord Rosebery's Escape from Houndsditch', *The Nineteenth Century*, 1901, reprinted in E.J.T. Brennan, ed., *Education for National Efficiency*, London, 1975, pp. 79–80.

10. Webb, ibid., pp. 18–19; Webb, cited in Simon, *Education and the Labour Movement*, p. 206.

11. Antonio Gramsci, *Selections from the Prison Notebooks*, ed. Quintin Hoare and Geoffrey Nowell-Smith, London, 1971, p. 247.

12. M. Seaborne, *The English School: Its Architecture and Organization 1807–1870*, London, 1971, pp. 137–9.

13. Michel Foucault, *Discipline and Punish: The Birth of the Prison*, London, 1977, p. 172.

14. Kay-Shuttleworth, cited in Hunter, *Culture and Government*, pp. 39–40. See also David Hamilton, 'On Simultaneous Instruction and the Early Evolution of Class Teaching', in *Towards a Theory of Schooling*, Lewes, 1989, pp. 99ff.; Hunter, *Culture and Government* p. 62; Dave Jones, 'The Genealogy of the Urban Schoolteacher', in Stephen J. Ball, ed., *Foucault and Education: Disciplines and Knowledge*, London, 1990.

15. Seaborne, *The English School*, p. 144.

16. Hamilton 'On Simultaneous Instruction', pp. 106–7; Stow, cited in Hunter, *Culture and Government*, p. 17.

17. M. Seaborne and R. Lowe, *The English School: Its Architecture and Organization, vol. 2 1870–1970*, London, 1977, pp. 25, 29–30.

18. Cited in Jones, 'The Genealogy', p. 58; Hunter, *Culture and Government*, pp. 52, 35, 17, 63–4.

19. On classroom teachers, Jones, 'The Genealogy', p. 62; on the new pedagogy, Hamilton, pp. 111–13.

20. Walkerdine, 'Developmental Psychology'.

21. On the archive, see Carlo Ginzburg, 'Morelli, Freud and Sherlock Holmes: Clues and Scientific Method', *History Workshop Journal*, no. 9, 1980, p. 24; Foucault, *Discipline and Punish*, p. 191; John Tagg, 'Power and Photography', *Screen Education*, no. 36, 1980 (Barnardo's cited pp. 43–4). On the London Visitors, see David Rubinstein, 'The London School Board, 1870–1904', in Peter McCann, ed., *Popular Education and Socialization in the Nineteenth Century*, London, 1977, pp. 232–3; on truancy (in the Scottish context), Fiona M.S. Paterson, 'Schooling the Family', *Sociology*, vol. 22, no. 1, February 1988, 65–86.

22. Foucault, *Power/Knowledge*, p. 209.

23. Lowe cited in Simon, *The Two Nations*, p. 356.

24. Michel Foucault, 'The Order of Discourse', in Robert Young, ed., *Untying the Text*, London, 1981, p. 64. On classification and framing, see, for example, Basil Bernstein, *Class, Codes and Control* vol. 3, 2nd edn, London, 1977; and 'Codes, Modalities and the Process of Cultural Reproduction: A Model', in Michael W. Apple, ed., *Cultural and Economic Reproduction in Education*, London, 1982.

25. See Rose, 'Governing the Enterprising Self', pp. 24–5; Jacqueline Rose, 'Femininity and its Discontents', *Feminist Review*, no. 14, 1983, p. 9; Joan Copjec, 'The Orthopsychic Subject: Film Theory and the Reception of Lacan', *October*, no. 49, 1989, p. 62.

2. How English Is It?

1. The epigraph from Said is in *The World, the Text, and the Critic*, London, 1984, p. 169. See also Eric Hobsbawm and Terence Ranger, eds, *The Invention of Tradition*, Cambridge, 1983; and Robert Colls and Philip Dodd, eds, *Englishness: Politics and Culture 1880–1920*, London, 1986, especially the chapter 'The Invention of English' by Brian Doyle. On Literature as an organizing category, see Tony Bennett, 'Marxism and Popular Fiction', *Literature and History*, vol. 7, no. 2, Autumn 1981, p. 7.

2. Michel de Certeau, *The Practice of Everyday Life*, Berkeley, 1984, p. xv. pp. 169, xxi.

3. Said, *The World*, p. 8; Benedict Anderson, *Imagined Communities: Reflections on the Origin and Spread of Nationalism*, London, 1983.

4. John Maynard Keynes, 'The Arts Council: Its Policy and Hopes', *The Listener*, no. 34, 12 July 1945.

5. Such work was pioneered in France by Renée Balibar and her colleagues. For examples of British work influenced by this approach, see Tony Davies,

'Education, Ideology and Literature', *Red Letters*, no. 7, 1978; Brian Doyle, 'The Hidden History of English Studies', in Peter Widdowson, ed., *Re-Reading English*, London, 1982; and 'The Invention of English'; Jacqueline Rose, *The Case of Peter Pan or the Impossibility of Children's Fiction*, London, 1984, ch. 5: 'Peter Pan, Language and the State: Captain Hook Goes to Eton'.

6. See my 'How Literacy Became a Problem (And Illiteracy Stopped Being One)', *Journal of Education*, vol. 165, no. 1, Winter 1983; Jane Mackay and Pat Thane, 'The Englishwoman', in Colls and Dodd, *Englishness*, p. 193.

7. See, for example, Michael Denning, *Mechanic Accents: Dime Novels and Working-class Culture in America*, London, 1987, especially chs 3–5.

8. Fredric Jameson, 'Reification and Utopia in Mass Culture', *Social Text*, no. 1, Winter 1979, p. 133; Laura Kipnis, '"Refunctioning" Reconsidered: Towards a Left Popular Culture', in Colin MacCabe, ed., *High Theory/Low Taste: Analysing Popular Television and Film*, Manchester, 1986, p. 22. (Where the real *need* for the modernism/mass culture binarism lies is, I suspect, indicated by the quotation from Laura Kipnis. It is necessary primarily so that the argument that postmodernism explodes the polarity can make sense.)

9. Peter Brooker and Peter Widdowson, 'A Literature for England', in Colls and Dodd, *Englishness*, p. 153.

10. This perspective is well exemplified in the articles by Ian Hunter, Colin Mercer and Tony Bennett, in *New Formations*, no. 4, Spring 1988. See also Hunter's 'After Representation: Recent Discussions of the Relation between Language and Literature , *Economy and Society*, vol. 13, no. 4, November 1984; and Mercer's 'That's Entertainment: The Resilience of Popular Forms', in Tony Bennett, Colin Mercer and Janet Woollacott, eds, *Popular Culture and Social Relations*, Milton Keynes, 1986.

11. Peter Stallybrass and Allon White, *The Politics and Poetics of Transgression*, London, 1986, p. 5.

12. Ibid., p. 193; Edward Said, *Orientalism*, New York, 1979, pp. 3, 7.

13. de Certeau, pp. 172, 174.

14. Sax Rohmer, *The Mystery of Dr. Fu Manchu*, London, 1985 [1913], p. 19. Further page references are given in the text.

15. Freud's reference to the novelette form of reverie as both stereotyped and variable, and therefore as the model fantasy, is taken up by Jean Laplanche and J.-B. Pontalis, 'Fantasy and the Origins of Sexuality', in Victor Burgin, James Donald and Cora Kaplan, eds, *Formations of Fantasy*, London, 1986, p. 22. For an attempt to give a historical context for this cycle of literature in the United States, see R. Valerie Lucas, 'Yellow Peril in the Promised Land: The Representation of the Oriental and the Question of American Identity', in Francis Barker, Peter Hulme, Margaret Iversen and Diana Loxley, eds, *Europe and its Others*, vol. 1, Colchester, 1985. On the change from the adventure story to the thriller: Michael Denning, *Cover Stories: Narrative and Ideology in the British Spy Thriller*, London, 1987, p. 41.

16. Julia Kristeva, *Powers of Horror: An Essay on Abjection*, New York, 1982, p. 4.

17. Sigmund Freud, 'Creative Writers and Day-dreaming' (1908), *The Pelican Freud Library*, vol. 14, Harmondsworth, 1985, p. 138.

18. Sigmund Freud, 'A Child Is Being Beaten (A Contribution to the Study of the Origins of Sexual Perversions)' (1919), *Penguin Freud Library*, vol. 10, Harmondsworth, 1979. Laplanche and Pontalis, 'Fantasy and the Origins of Sexuality', pp. 22–3.

19. Stephen Heath, 'Psychopathia Sexualis: Stevenson's *Strange Case*', *Critical Quarterly*, vol. 28, nos. 1/2, 1986, pp. 98, 100, 103, 104, 104/5.

20. Pierre Bourdieu, *Distinction: A Social Critique of the Judgement of Taste*, London, 1984, p. 33; Roland Barthes, *Mythologies*, London, 1972, p. 21. See also Valerie Walkerdine's reading of *Rocky IV*: 'Video Replay: Families, Films and Fantasy', in Burgin, Donald and Kaplan, *Formations of Fantasy*.

21. Slavoj Žižck, *The Sublime Object of Ideology*, London, 1989, p. 110.

22. A reference to Klaus Theweleit's formulation in *Male Fantasies*, Cambridge, 1987, p. 428.

23. Walter Abish, *How German Is It?*, London, 1983; 'The English Garden', in *In the Future Perfect*, London, 1984, p. 1.

24. Adapted from Victor Burgin, 'Diderot, Barthes, *Vertigo*', in Burgin, Donald and Kaplan, *Formations of Fantasy*, p. 98.

25. Paul Gilroy, *There Ain't No Black in the Union Jack*, London, 1987, pp. 12, 247.

26. Jacqueline Rose, 'The State of the Subject (II): The Institution of Feminism', *Critical Quarterly*, vol. 29, no. 4, 1987, pp. 13–14.

3. The Machinery of Democracy

1. Jones, quoted in Peter Gordon and John White, *Philosophers as Educational Reformers: The Influence of Idealism on British Educational Thought and Practice*, London, 1979, pp. 192–4.

2. Herbert Read, *Education through Art*, London, 1943, 3rd revised edn [1956], p. 5.

3. This section draws on Francis Mulhern, *The Moment of 'Scrutiny'*, London, 1979, pp. 35ff.

4. Lord Reith, *Into the Wind*, London, 1949, p. 136. See also Simon Frith, 'The Pleasures of the Hearth', in *Formations of Pleasure*, London, 1983.

5. See Stuart Hood, 'John Grierson and the Documentary Film Movement', in James Curran and Vincent Porter, eds, *British Cinema History*, London, 1983.

6. John Grierson, *Grierson on Documentary*, ed. Forsyth Hardy, London, 1966, p. 78; *Broadcasting and the Cinema as Instruments of Education* London, 1936.

7. Grierson, *Grierson on Documentary*, p. 95; *Broadcasting and the Cinema*.

8. On Thompson, see Brian Doyle, 'Some Uses of English: Denys Thompson and the Development of English in Secondary Schools', Centre for Contemporary Cultural Studies Stencilled Occasional Paper, University of Birmingham, 1981. On Richards: John Bowen, 'I.A. Richards – A Mechanic of the Subject', *Literature and History: Education Issue*, Spring 1987.

9. Margaret McMillan, *Education through the Imagination*, London, 1904, pp. 26, 58–9, 13; cited in Ian Hunter, *Culture and Government*, pp. 116–17.

10. On Newbolt, see Hunter, *Culture and Government*, pp. 120–32; Noel King, 'The Newbolt Report Re-examined', *Literature and History: Education Issue*, Spring 1987; Brian Doyle, *English and Englishness*, London, 1989.

11. On psychology as a normative discipline in this period, see Walkerdine, 'Developmental Psychology and the Child-centred Pedagogy', in Julian Henriques, Wendy Hollway, Cathy Urwin, Couze Venn and Valerie Walkerdine, *Changing the Subject*, London, 1984; Nikolas Rose, *The Psychological Complex: Psychology, Politics and Society in England 1869–1939*, London, 1985; and Denise Riley, *War in the Nursery: Theories of the Child and the Mother*, London, 1983.

12. See Lesley Johnson, 'Radio and Everyday Life: The Early Years of Broadcasting in Australia 1922–1945', *Media, Culture and Society*, vol. 3, 1981; Paddy Scannell and David Cardiff, 'Serving the Nation: Public Service Broadcasting before the War', in Bernard Waites, Tony Bennett and Graham Martin, eds, *Popular Culture: Past and Present*, London, 1982, pp. 168–9; David Cardiff, 'The Serious and the Popular: Aspects of the Evolution of Style in the Radio Talk 1928–1939', *Media, Culture and Society*, vol. 2, 1980, p. 30.

13. Reith, *Into the Wind*, p. 100; Paddy Scannell, 'Public Service Broadcasting and Modern Public Life', *Media, Culture and Society*, vol. 11, 1989, p. 149; Frith, 'The Pleasures of the Hearth', p. 115; Bill Schwarz, 'The Language of Constitutionalism: Baldwinite Conservatism', in *Formations of Nation and People*, London, 1984, p. 9.

14. H. Jennings and W. Gill, *Broadcasting and Everyday Life: A Survey of the Social Effects of the Coming of Broadcasting*, London, 1939, p. 17; quoted in Shaun Moores, '"The Box on the Dresser": Memories of Early Radio and Everyday Life', *Media, Culture and Society*, vol. 10, 1988, p. 34.

15. See Scannell, 'Public Service Broadcasting', pp. 139–41.

16. Cardiff, 'The Serious and the Popular', pp. 35–6; Paddy Scannell, 'Music for the Multitude? The Dilemmas of the BBC's Music Policy 1923–1946', *Media, Culture and Society*, vol. 3, 1981; Jody Berland, 'Radio Space and Industrial Time: Music Formats, Local Narratives and Technological Mediation', *Popular Music*, vol. 9, no. 2, 1990.

17. Colin Mercer, 'That's Entertainment: The Resilence of Popular Forms', in Tony Bennett, Colin Mercer and Janet Woollacott, eds, *Popular Culture and Social Relations*, Milton Keynes, 1986, p. 193; Grierson, *Grierson on Documentary*, p. 77; Robert Colls and Philip Dodd, 'Representing the Nation – British Documentary Film 1930–45', *Screen*, vol. 26, no. 1, January–February 1985, p. 23.

18. Grierson, *Grierson on Documentary*, pp. 100, 68–9; The Arts Enquiry, *The Factual Film: A Survey*, Oxford, 1947, p. 59; John M. MacKenzie, *Propaganda and Empire*, Manchester, 1984, p. 87; Grierson, *Grierson on Documentary*, p. 217. For an excellent account of the arrival of television in American homes in the post-war period, see Lynn Spigel, 'Installing the Television Set: Popular Discourses on Television and Domestic Space 1948–1955', *Camera Obscura*, no. 16, 1988.

4. Strutting and Fretting

1. See Andreas Huyssen, 'The Vamp and the Machine: Fritz Lang's *Metropolis*', in *After the Great Divide: Modernism, Mass Culture, Postmodernism*, Bloomington, 1986; and also Peter Wollen, 'Cinema/Americanism/the Robot', in *New Formations*, no. 8, 1989.

2. Rousseau cited in Adrian Oldfield, 'Citizenship: An Unnatural Practice?', *Political Quarterly*, vol. 61, no. 2, 1990, p. 186; Donna Haraway, 'A Manifesto for Cyborgs: Science, Technology, and Socialist Feminism in the 1980s', *Socialist Review*, vol. 80, 1985, pp. 65, 66; Foucault, *Power/Knowledge*, p. 186; Gilles Deleuze, *Foucault*, Minneapolis, 1988, p. 115.

3. Ian Hunter, *Culture and Government*, London, 1988, pp. 150, 125; Nikolas Rose, *Governing the Soul*, London, 1990, p. 208.

4. Ian Hunter, 'After Representation: Recent Discussions of the Relation between Language and Literature', *Economy* and *Society*, vol. 13, no. 4, November 1984, p. 423; Rose, *Governing the Soul*, p. 218.

5. Rose, *Governing the Soul*, pp. 201–2.

6. The definition of repression is taken from Mark Cousins and Athar Hussain, *Michel Foucault*, London, 1984. p. 208. On the distinction between the subject as an effect of the law and the realization of the law, see Joan Copjec, 'The Orthopsychic Subject: Film Theory and the Reception of Lacan', *October*, no. 49, 1989, p. 61. My general argument here also borrows from this article, as well as others by Copjec. See, for example, 'The Delirium of Clinical Perfection', *Oxford Literary Review*, vol. 8, nos 1–2, 1986, and 'Cutting Up', in Teresa Brennan, ed., *Between Feminism and Psychoanalysis*, London 1989. On the link to Mauss, see Cousins, 'In the Midst of Psychoanalysis', *New Formations*, no. 7, Spring 1989, p 79

7. Claude Lévi-Strauss, *Introduction to the Work of Marcel Mauss*, London 1987, p. 35 (see also Homi Bhabha, 'DissemiNation', in Bhabha, ed., *Nation and Narration*, London, 1990, p. 313). Jacques Lacan, *The Four Fundamental Concepts of Psycho-analysis*, London, 1977, p. 56.

8. Copjec, 'The Orthopsychic Subject', p. 70.

9. See, for example, Valerie Walkerdine, *The Mastery of Reason: Cognitive Development and the Production of Rationality*, London, 1988; Walkerdine and the Girls and Mathematics Unit, Institute of Education, *Counting Girls Out*, London, 1989; Walkerdine and Helen Lucey, *Democracy in the Kitchen: Regulating Mothers and Socializing Daughters*, London, 1989.

5. What's at Stake in Vampire Films?

1. Sigmund Freud, *The Standard Edition of the Complete Psychological Works*, vol. 1, ed. James Strachey, London, 1953–66, p. 243. Otto Rank, *The Double: A Psychoanalytic Study*, London, 1989, pp. 3–4.

2. Julia Kristeva, *Powers of Horror: An Essay on Abjection*, New York, 1982, p. 11.

3. Franco Moretti, 'Dialectic of Fear', in *Signs Taken for Wonders*, London, 1983, p. 105. Robin Wood, 'An Introduction to the American Horror Film', in Bill Nichols, ed., *Movies and Methods*, vol. 2, Berkeley, 1985, pp. 201, 203.

4. Moretti, 'Dialectic of Fear', p. 108; Wood, 'The American Horror Film', p. 196. Fredric Jameson, 'Magical Narratives: On the Dialectical Use of Genre Criticism', in *The Political Unconscious: Narrative as a Socially Symbolic Act*, London, 1981, p. 115.

5. Tzvetan Todorov, *The Fantastic: A Structural Approach to a Literary Genre*, Ithaca, NY, 1973, pp. 25, 120.

6. See Mark Nash, '*Vampyr* and the Fantastic', *Screen*, vol. 17, no. 3, Autumn 1976; and David Bordwell, *The Films of Carl-Theodor Dreyer*, Berkeley, 1981. Todorov, *The Fantastic*, p. 168.

7. Thomas Elsaesser, 'Social Mobility and the Fantastic: German Silent Cinema', in James Donald, ed., *Fantasy and the Cinema*, London, 1989, p. 31; Constance Penley, 'Time Travel, Primal Scene and the Critical Dystopia', ibid., p. 197.

8. Freud, 'The "Uncanny"' (1919), *Art and Literature, The Penguin Freud Library*, vol. 14, Harmondsworth, 1985, p. 373.

9. Ibid., p. 354. For a useful summary of the critiques of Freud on *The Sandman*, see Elizabeth Wright, *Psychoanalytic Criticism: Theory in Practice*, London, 1984, pp. 142ff.

10. Hélène Cixous, 'Fiction and its Phantoms: A Reading of Freud's *Das Unheimliche* ("The Uncanny")', *New Literary History*, vol. 7, Spring 1976, pp. 540, 543, 544, 545.

11. See Harold Bloom, 'Freud and the Sublime: A Catastrophe Theory of Creativity', in *Agon*, Oxford, 1982.

12. Edmund Burke, *A Philosophical Enquiry into the Origin of our Ideas of the Sublime and Beautiful* [1757], ed. James T. Boulton, London, 1958, p. 58.

13. Here and in the following paragraphs I draw extensively on Paul Crowther, 'The Kantian Sublime, the Avant-garde, and the Postmodern: A Critique of Lyotard', *New Formations*, no. 7, Spring 1989.

14. On the Gothic novel, see Mario Praz, *The Romantic Agony* [1933], London, 1970; on its relationship to horror films, see David Pirie, *A Heritage of Horror: The English Gothic Cinema 1946–1972*, London, 1973; and S.S. Prawer, *Caligari's Children: The Film as Tale of Terror*, Oxford, 1980. On Walpole, David Morris, 'Gothic Sublimity', *New Literary History*, vol. XVI, no. 2, Winter 1985, p. 311.

15. Peter Brooks, *The Melodramatic Imagination*, New York 1985, pp. 20, 5.

16. Kristeva, *Powers of Horror*, pp. 4, 2, 9–10, 12. On Foucault, see Scott Lash, 'Postmodernity and Desire', *Theory and Society*, no. 14, 1985, pp. 4, 8.

17. Julia Kristeva, 'Ellipsis on Dread and the Specular Seduction', *Wide Angle*, vol. 3, no. 3, 1979, pp. 44, 46. On modernism and kitsch, John Rajchman, *Michel Foucault: The Freedom of Philosophy*, New York, 1985, pp. 17–18.

18. My account of Lyotard's sublime borrows from Crowther, 'The Kantian

Sublime'; Meaghan Morris, 'Postmodernity and Lyotard's Sublime', *Art & Text*, no. 16, Summer 1984/5; and David Carroll, 'Rephrasing the Political with Kant and Lyotard: From Aesthetic to Political Judgments', *Diacritics*, Fall 1984.

19. Jean-François Lyotard, *The Postmodern Condition: A Report on Knowledge*, Manchester, 1984, p. 67.

20. Carroll, 'Rephrasing the Political', pp. 83–4.

21. On Lyotard's view of popular culture, see his bemused response to three papers at an ICA event in London, 1985, which he found 'a little hasty with their concessions to what is positive in these forms of pop culture or mass culture', and suggests as an alternative television programmes or whatever which 'produce in the viewer or the client in general an effect of uncertainty and trouble'. Lisa Appignanesi, ed., *Postmodernism: ICA Documents 4/5*, London 1986, p. 58. On the popular tradition of narration, Jean-François Lyotard and Jean-Loup Thébaud, *Just Gaming*, Manchester, 1985, pp. 32, 33; also David Carroll, 'Narrative, Heterogeneity, and the Question of the Political: Bakhtin and Lyotard', in Murray Krieger, ed., *The Aims of Representation: Subject/Text/History*, New York, 1987, pp. 100–1.

22. Sarah Benton, 'Monsters from the Deep', *New Statesman*, 19 October 1984, quoted in Jacqueline Rose, 'Margaret Thatcher and Ruth Ellis', *New Formations*, no. 6, Winter 1988/9, p. 27n; Laura Mulvey, 'Changes: Thoughts on Myth, Narrative and Historical Experience', *History Workshop Journal*, no. 23, London, 1987, p. 5; Michael Rogin, *Ronald Reagan, the Movie, and other Episodes in Political Demonology*, Berkeley, 1987, p. xiii; Rose, 'Margaret Thatcher and Ruth Ellis', p. 17.

23. Saul Friedländer, *Reflections of Nazism: An Essay on Kitsch and Death*, New York, 1984, pp. 19, 130–1. Lyotard, cited in Carroll, 'Narrative, Heterogeneity', p. 106.

24. See, for example, Pierre Bourdieu, *Distinction: A Social Critique of the Judgement of Taste*, London, 1984.

25. Antonio Gramsci, *Selections from The Prison Notebooks*, London, 1971, p. 276; Klaus Theweleit, *Male Fantasies*, Cambridge, 1987.

26. Frantz Fanon, *The Wretched of the Earth*, Harmondsworth, 1967, pp. 182–3, cited in Homi K. Bhabha, 'The Commitment to Theory', *New Formations*, no. 5, Summer 1988, p. 19.

27. On the popular consumption of symbolic forms, see Michel de Certeau, *The Practice of Everyday Life*, Berkeley, 1984; on the political possibilities of boundary transgression and reconstruction, see Donna Haraway, 'A Manifesto for Cyborgs', *Socialist Review*, vol. 80, 1985.

6. Mrs Thatcher's Legacy

1. See Peter Golding and Graham Murdock, 'Pulling the Plugs on Democracy', *New Statesman*, 30 June 1989.

2. Roger Scruton, *The Meaning of Conservatism*, Harmondsworth, 1980, pp. 158–9.

3. Richard Collins, 'White and Green and Not Much Read', *Screen*, vol. 30, nos. 1/2, 1989.

4. See Martin McLean, 'The Conservative Education Policy in Comparative Perspective: Return to an English Golden Age or Harbinger of International Policy Change?', *British Journal of Educational Studies*, vol. xxxvi, no. 3, 1988.

5. Colin Gordon, 'The Soul of the Citizen: Max Weber and Michel Foucault in Rationality and Government', in Sam Whimster and Scott Lash, eds, *Max Weber, Rationality and Modernity*, London, 1987, p. 297.

6. Denis Lawton, *Education, Culture and the National Curriculum*, London, 1989, p. 52.

7. Raymond Williams, *The Long Revolution*, Harmondsworth, 1965, pp. 173–6; David Hargreaves, *The Challenge for the Comprehensive School: Culture, Curriculum and Community*, London, 1982, pp. 161ff, 213–14.

8. For critiques of Williams, see Ian Hunter, *Culture and Government*, London, 1988; and Paul Gilroy, *There Ain't No Black in the Union Jack*, London, 1987, pp. 49ff.

9. John Mortimer, 'The Murder of British Television: A Whydunnit', *Samizdat*, no. 2, January/February 1989, pp. 7–8. On the regulation of commercial television, see Norman Lewis, 'If You See Dicey Will You Tell Him? Regulatory Problems in British Constitutional Law', *The Political Quarterly*, p. 17. My critique here draws on John Keane, '"Liberty of the Press" in the 1990s', *New Formations*, no. 8, Summer 1989.

10. See, for example, Stuart Hall, 'The State – Socialism's Old Caretaker', in *The Hard Road to Renewal*, London, 1988; John Keane, *Democracy and Civil Society*, London, 1988, ch. 1.

11. See especially Centre for Contemporary Cultural Studies, *Unpopular Education*, London, 1981.

12. See, for example, Ernesto Laclau and Chantal Mouffe, *Hegemony and Socialist Strategy: Towards a Radical Democratic Politics*, London, 1985, esp. p. 176; Mouffe, 'The Civics Lesson', *New Statesman and Society*, 7 October 1988; and 'Radical Democracy: Modern or Postmodern?', in Andrew Ross, ed., *Universal Abandon? The Politics of Postmodernism*, Edinburgh, 1989; David Held, *Models of Democracy*, Cambridge, 1987; Stuart Hall and David Held, 'Left and Rights', *Marxism Today*, June 1989.

13. See, for example, Mouffe, 'The Civics Lesson' and 'Radical Democracy'; Quentin Skinner, 'The Idea of Negative Liberty: Philosophical and Historical Perspectives', and Charles Taylor, 'Philosophy and its History', both in Richard Rorty, J.B. Schneewind and Quentin Skinner, eds, *Philosophy in History*, Cambridge, 1984.

14. John Rajchman, *Michel Foucault: The Freedom of Philosophy*, New York, 1985, pp. 59–60; Onora O'Neill, *Constructions of Reasons: Explorations of Kant's Practical Philosophy*, Cambridge, 1989, chs 1 and 2.

15. This definition is adapted from Nicholas Garnham, 'Public Service versus the Market', *Screen*, vol. 24, no. 1, 1983, p. 14. See also Paddy Scannell, 'Public Service Broadcasting and Modern Public Life, *Media, Culture and Society*, vol. 11, 1989; and Keane, '"Liberty of the Press"'.

16. Scannell, 'Public Service Broadcasting', p. 137.

17. Claude Lefort, *The Political Forms of Modern Society*, Cambridge, 1986, pp. 279, 305; Scannell, 'Public Service Broadcasting', p. 161.

18. See Franco Bianchini, 'GLC R.I.P: Cultural Policies in London, 1981–1986', *New Formations*, no. 1, 1987, esp. pp. 111–14.

19. Roger Silverstone, 'Let us then Return to the Murmuring of Everyday Practices: A Note on Michel de Certeau, Television and Everyday Life', *Theory, Culture & Society*, vol. 6, no. 1, 1989, pp. 86, 88.

20. de Certeau, *The Practice of Everyday Life*, p. 31.

7. Diagrams of Citizenship

1. Alasdair MacIntyre, 'The Idea of an Educated Public', in Graham Haydon, ed., *Education and Values*, London, 1987, pp. 24–5.

2. Nikolas Rose, 'Governing the Enterprising Self', paper for *The Values of the Enterprise Culture*, University of Lancaster, September 1989, p. 4. On states that are essentially a by-product, see Renata Salecl, 'Homage to the Great Other', *Prose Studies*, vol. 11, no. 3, December 1988, pp. 89ff; she adapts the concept from Jon Elster, *Sour Grapes: Studies in the Subversion of Rationality*, Cambridge, 1983.

3. Chantal Mouffe, 'The Civics Lesson', *New Statesman and Society*, 7 October 1988, p. 31; Michael Walzer, *Spheres of Justice*, New York, 1983, p. 208.

4. Amy Gutmann, *Democratic Education*, Princeton, 1987, pp. 71, 74.

5. Raymond Williams, *The Long Revolution*, Harmondsworth, 1965, pp. 173–6.

6. John Henry Newman, *The Idea of a University*, ed. I.T. Ker, Oxford, 1976, pp. 136, 146, 154.

7. For useful critiques of Wiener, see John Ahier, *Industry, Children and the Nation*, Lewes, 1988; and Paul Hirst, *After Thatcher*, London, 1989, pp. 120ff.

8. Newman, *The Idea*, pp. 154–5.

9. F.R. Leavis, *Education and the University: A Sketch for an 'English School'*, revised edn, London 1948 [1943], pp. 16, 23, 24, 28, 30.

10. Quoted in Brian Doyle, *English and Englishness*, London, 1989, p. 99.

11. Martin Trow, 'The Robbins Trap: British Attitudes and the Limits of Expansion', *Higher Education Quarterly*, vol. 43, no. 1, 1988, p. 62. See also Michael Rustin, 'Comprehensive Education after 18', in *For a Pluralist Socialism*, London, 1985.

12. Lenin, cited in Nigel Grant, *Soviet Education*, London, 1964, pp. 29–30, and in Martin Hoyles, ed., *The Politics of Literacy*, London, 1977, p. 20.

13. E.D. Hirsch, Jr, *Cultural Literacy: What Every American Needs to Know*, Boston, 1987; Allan Bloom, *The Closing of the American Mind*, Harmondsworth, 1988.

14. Ibid., pp. 27, 53.

15. Ibid., pp. xiii–xv.

16. Ibid., pp. 2, 22; T.S. Eliot, *Notes Towards the Definition of Culture*, London, 1963 [1948], p. 100.

17. Renée Balibar, *Les Français Fictifs*, Paris, 1974.

18. Gauri Viswanathan, 'The Beginnings of English Literary Study in British India', *Oxford Literary Review*, vol. 9, 1987. Homi K. Bhabha, 'Of Mimicry and Man: The Ambivalence of Colonial Discourse', *October*, no. 28, 1984. Their approach suggests a more nuanced map of class differentiation than Balibar's rather schematic version, with a special emphasis on the formation of a petty bourgeoisie in the metropolitan societies.

19. ILEA Centre for Language in Primary Education, *The Primary Language Record: A Handbook for Teachers*, London, 1989, p. 24. I am grateful to Jay Snow for introducing me to this document, and for his helpful reading of it.

20. Ibid., pp. 38, 22.

21. Dixon, cited in Ian Hunter, *Culture and Government*, London, 1988, pp. 16–17.

22. *PLR*, pp. 14, 15.

23. Antonio Gramsci, *Selections from the Prison Notebooks*, London, 1971, pp. 35–6. See also Jonathan Steinberg, 'The Historian and the *questione della lingua*', in Peter Burke and Roy Porter, eds, *The Social History of Language*, Cambridge, 1987, p. 205.

24. Raymond Williams, *The Country and the City*, London, 1973, p. 84.

25. In a discussion, Margaret Meek pointed out to me that one of the virtues of the *Primary Literacy Record* is that its production involved the reflections and insights of many teachers, thus changing their relation to their own work and the terms of their participation in it.

26. Robert Moore, 'Education and the Ideology of Production', *British Journal of Sociology of Education*, vol. 8, no. 2, 1987, p. 241.

27. See Hirst, *After Thatcher*, p. 198; David Finegold and David Soskice, 'The Failure of Training in Britain: Analysis and Prescription', *Oxford Journal of Economic Policy*, vol. 4, no. 3, Autumn 1988.

28. See Ken Spours and Michael Young, *Beyond Vocationalism: A New Perspective on the Relationship between Work and Education*, Working Paper no. 4, London, Institute of Education Post-16 Education Centre, 1988, p. 11; John Ahier, 'Explaining Economic Decline and Teaching Children about Industry: Some Unintended Continuities?', unpublished ms, August 1989; Geoff Esland, ed., *Education, Training and Employment*, 2 vols, Wokingham, 1990.

29. Thomas J. Peters and Robert H. Waterman, Jr, *In Search of Excellence: Lessons from America's Best Run Companies*, London, 1982; Rose, *Governing the Soul*, pp. 113–15. I am grateful to Paul du Gay for his guidance in this area.

30. Sabrina Broadbent and Ros Moger, 'But Is It English ...? The National Curriculum and Progressive English Teaching', in Peter Brooker and Peter Humm, eds, *Dialogue and Difference: English into the Nineties*, London, 1989, p. 47.

31. Gutmann, *Democratic Education*, p. 51.

32. Alasdair MacIntyre, *Whose Justice? Which Rationality?*, London, 1988, p. 388.

33. For a political programme along such lines, see Raymond Plant, *Citizenship, Rights and Socialism*, London, 1988.

34. Gutmann, *Democratic Education*, esp. pp. 16ff.

35. See Claude Lefort, *The Political Forms of Modern Society*, Cambridge, 1986, p. 279; Ernesto Laclau and Chantal Mouffe, *Hegemony and Socialist Strategy*, London, 1985, p. 190.

Coda: The Happiest Time . . .

1. Gustave Flaubert, *Sentimental Education*, trans. Robert Baldrick, Harmondsworth, 1968, pp. 415, 418–19.

2. My reading of Dewey draws on J.E. Tiles, *Dewey*, London, 1988, esp. ch. IX, 'Ideals'.

3. Richard Rorty, *Consequences of Pragmatism*, Brighton, 1982, pp. 207, 208.

4. Tiles, *Dewey*, pp. 211, 214.

5. John Dewey, *The Public and its Problems*, New York, 1927, p. 216; Rorty, *Consequences*, p. 205.

6. Tiles, *Dewey*, pp. 219–21.

7. Gilles Deleuze, *Foucault*, Minneapolis, 1988, p. 89; Donna Haraway, 'A Manifesto for Cyborgs: Science, Technology, and Socialist Feminism in the 1980s', *Socialist Review*, vol. 80, 1985.

INDEX